READY TO READ

A Parents' Guide

MARY ANN DZAMA and ROBERT GILSTRAP
GEORGE MASON UNIVERSITY

A VOLUME IN THE
WILEY PARENT EDUCATION SERIES
MARK A. SPIKELL, EDITOR

A WILEY PRESS BOOK

JOHN WILEY & SONS, INC.
NEW YORK • CHICESTER • BRISBANE • TORONTO • SINGAPORE

THIS BOOK IS DEDICATED
TO
OUR PARENTS
WHO INSTILLED IN US
A LOVE OF READING
WHICH WE HAVE HAD OPPORTUNITIES
TO SHARE WITH OTHER PARENTS
AND THEIR CHILDREN

Copyright © 1983 by John Wiley & Sons, Inc.

All rights reserved. Published simultaneously in Canada.

Reproduction or translation of any part of this work beyond that permitted by Section 107 or 108 of the 1976 United States Copyright Act without the permission of the copyright owner is unlawful. Requests for permission or further information should be addressed to the Permissions Department, John Wiley & Sons, Inc.

Library of Congress Cataloging in Publication Data

Dzama, Mary Ann, 1942–
    Ready to read.

    (Wiley parent education series)
    Bibliography: p.
    Includes index.
    1. Reading readiness. 2. Reading (Preschool)
3. Reading (Primary) I. Gilstrap, Robert. II. Title.
III. Series.
LB1181.35.D93   1983   372.4   82-24777

ISBN: 0-471-86637-7

Printed in the United States of America
83 84 10 9 8 7 6 5 4 3 2 1

Acknowledgements and Copyright Notices

Although many people provided us with assistance during the writing of this guide for parents, we would like to give special recognition to the following:
• Mark Spikell, the series editor, who guided us through the entire process from idea to final publication.
• Our students at George Mason University, especially those involved in the graduate reading program.
• The parents and children who have utilized the services of the George Mason Child/Youth Study Center.
• The faculty, especially those who read initial drafts of specialized material.
• Ann Byrnes, our illustrator.
• Our typists, especially Jane Payne, Diane Wallace, Anne Bauman, and Rose Medford, who did most of the typing.
• The parents of April Doebler and Thea Van Sickle for allowing us to use their art work.
• Our friends and families, especially Dorothy Barclay Gilstrap who provided invaluable assistance throughout the development of the book.
Grateful acknowledgement is also made to the following for permission to use materials owned by them. If any holders of rights have been inadvertently overlooked, the authors offer apologies and the promise of correction in later editions:

CONTENTS

Introduction

Most parents want their children to become good readers as early as possible. Reading is valued in our society and rightly so. It is an important skill that is basic to one's education. Some parents are often anxious and confused, however, about what role they should play in this process, especially before the child enters school. Should they teach their baby to read, as some experts recommend, or should they do nothing until their child is in school, as others suggest? How much and what kind of help will be useful to the child in helping him or her become a confident and competent reader?

If you are a parent of a preschool or primary-school-age child and have asked yourself such questions and not found satisfactory answers, then this book is designed for you. Let us explain why.

First, this book is planned to help you better understand how your child develops from a crying infant into a confident eight-year-old who is reading his or her favorite books with ease. We believe that you as a parent need to know as much as possible about this process because it's a fascinating time in the development of your child and because this knowledge can be useful to you in being a more effective parent.

Second, this book contains information that should help you better understand the different points of view about what reading is and how it should be taught. You may have thought that there was only one way to define reading and one way to teach reading. Well, that's not the case, and we hope in this book to help you better understand what you might expect from the men and women who will be teaching your child to read. Since both of us have been public-school teachers and still work regularly with teachers and student teachers in schools, we are up to date on current practices. One of us works regularly with parents in a campus reading center, and the other, a parent of four children, educates teachers at undergraduate and graduate levels.

Finally, this book is designed to provide you with specific ideas for helping your child get ready to read and ways to assist your child once he or she moves into a formal reading program. These activities are not designed to teach your child to read but instead to *complement* the formal reading program that your child will move through in a school setting under the direction of a professional.

Although many readers of this book will be parents of young children, many others may be experienced parents who still have younger children at home. Such readers may have problems that might have been avoided or better understood if they had known more about the reading process and their important role during the preschool years. These readers might be interested in learning how to avoid repeating such problems with their younger children.

We do not believe that formal reading instruction must begin prior to first grade. Although some children are ready to read before first grade, most are not. We do believe, however, that children will have better attitudes toward reading and be more ready to begin formal reading instruction as a result of meaningful experiences provided by parents during the child's early years at home and in the neighborhood. We also believe that when this interest in the child's development continues into the primary grades, it enhances the child's growth as a reader, and current research supports this point of view.

WHAT'S IN THIS BOOK TO HELP YOUR CHILD GET READY TO READ?

There are some people who write about reading readiness who believe that one must have special programs for preschool children that focus on reading skills and that require large amounts of direct instruction on the part of the parent or the person caring for the child. We don't believe such programs are necessary or appropriate.

In this book we attempt to provide you with information about reading-readiness activities that are appropriate in working with your children during four major phases of their development:

1. The infant and toddler years (birth through age two)
2. The nursery-school years (ages three and four)
3. The kindergarten year (ages four and five)
4. The first-grade year (ages five and six).

Throughout the stages of a child's development, there are some basic activities that you as a parent can use to help your child get ready to read. They include talking with and listening to your child; reading to your child; being a reading model for your child; involving your child in a variety of recreational activities; and going places with your child.

Chapters 2 and 3 of this book will discuss how you can make the best use of your time with your child during his or her prekindergarten years. We will focus on the basic activities listed above and discuss specific activities that you and your child can enjoy. In choosing activities to include in this book, we've asked ourselves the following questions:

1. Do the activities provide an opportunity for children to experiment with language and to have fun with it?
2. Do they allow children to participate actively in the learning process rather than being passive recipients of knowledge?
3. Do they promote feelings of success in children and help them enjoy exploring language and learning to read?
4. Do they allow children to communicate what they know and how they feel?
5. Do they help show that reading experiences are part of a broader communication process that includes listening, speaking, and writing?

We think that the activities in this book merit "yes" answers to all five questions. (These five questions for selecting activities are adapted from a joint statement prepared by a group of professional organizations whose members are involved in prereading programs.)

In Chapter 4, we've tried to give a picture of how the different viewpoints of teachers about reading readiness can affect early school experiences. The chapter focuses on the kindergarten child and shows how what is being taught at school can be reinforced at home through games and other fun activities.

Chapter 5 describes the variety of reading programs used in the first grade. Although there is no national reading curriculum in the United States, reading programs throughout the country share many common elements, and we will share this information with you.

In Chapter 6, we've tried to address questions that we've been asked by parents in workshops and conference sessions at the Child/Youth Study Center at George Mason University. The questions cover a wide range of topics of special interest to many parents, and we hope you'll find this section helpful.

The final part of the book is a reference section that includes lists of favorite books for children, lists of selected free or inexpensive materials for parents, lists of magazines and newsletters from which you can get more information on reading, and a list of organizations for parents. What you have in your hands now is a useful resource for you throughout your child's early years. It will provide a sensible, natural approach that takes into consideration what is known about the development of the young child.

HOW TO USE THIS BOOK

This book has been written for all kinds of parents—first-time parents, last-time parents, and those who are any place in between.

If you are a first-time parent, we recommend that you use this book as a guide through your child's elementary-school years. You may want to read the whole book now to get a picture of the exciting processes that children go through as they become readers. Or you may prefer to read only this Introduction and the first chapter or two.

If you are an experienced parent with a new baby along with a child who is already reading, you may want to read the whole book to compare the activities recommended to the experiences you shared with your older child.

If your child is now somewhere in the middle of the childhood years, we recommend that you first focus on the chapter dealing with your child's current age, in order to gain a better understanding of the appropriate development of and activities for your child. Then go back to the beginning of the book to learn about what led up to this point.

In a nutshell, our goal with this book is to encourage parents to play a more active role in helping their children learn to read by providing information and activities that will help parents during their child's preschool and primary-grade years, not as the child's teacher, but as a partner in a cooperative venture.

1

THE PARENTS' ROLE IN THE READING PROCESS

Do you remember when you learned to read? It's hard to remember a time when you couldn't read, isn't it? Yet there was a time when words strung together in sentences meant nothing to you. And then came that magic moment when the words began to have meaning and you were able to read.

Miriam Cohen, one of our favorite writers for young children, has captured this moment in a picture book entitled *When Will I Read?* Jim, the central character, is a first-grader who wants very much to learn to read.

"You can read your name," Jim's teacher tells him.

"But that's not really reading," responds Jim.

"It will happen," she tells him. Jim is not convinced, however, and he's very concerned.

One day, Jim observes that the sign on the hamster cage has been ripped and now reads: "Do let the hamsters out." Jim rushes to his teacher to warn her about the sign, fearing that the hamsters could get killed.

She says, "We can fix that!" Then she smiles at Jim. "I told you it would happen," she says. "You can read."

"I waited all my life," Jim says. "Now I can read."

To many children, it does seem like a lifetime before they are able to read. They see others around them reading—their parents, older brothers and sisters—and they want to read as well. So when it finally happens, as it did to Jim, they breathe a sigh of relief: "Now I can read."

The anxiety that many children feel about learning to read was felt by a daughter of one of the authors. One day when Annie, age five, came home from school, she looked a bit worried, so her father invited her to sit down for a talk. He asked her how things were going in kindergarten. She told him about some of the activities that she liked best, then suddenly she asked, very seriously: "Do you think I'll be able to read by the time I'm in high school?"

When Annie's father asked her why she was concerned about learning to read, she explained that some children in her class already knew how to read. Although she was only in kindergarten, Annie was already feeling left behind.

Annie's father explained to her that some children do learn to read early, but most children learn to read in first grade, and some in second or even third grade, and that there was no doubt in his mind that Annie would learn to read long before high school. For Christmas Annie received a copy of *When Will I Read?* It helped her to understand that her time, like Jim's, would come. And during Annie's fourth month in first grade, it finally did.

But children like Annie are not the only ones who are anxious about learning to read. Many parents worry, too.

"A new burden has been added to the role of parent," says Caroline Zinsser, former director of New York's Bank Street School. "Now, in addition to food, clothes, shelter, love and friends, mothers and fathers are made to worry about 'cognitive stimulation.' " Ms. Zinsser is quoted by Carol Kruchoff in a *Washington Post* article, "Education: Pushing Kids to Success or Stress?" (Nov. 24, 1981). As the article explains, many child psychologists and family therapists are disturbed that parents are creating overly stressful situations for their children because these parents are "achievers" who want their children to be "achievers" as well. The first achievement sought by many of these parents is for their child to be the first on the block to read.

If you are reading this book in hopes of learning how to teach your child to read, you should return it now to the library or bookstore. That is *not* our purpose. There are already enough books that try to convince parents they should teach their preschool children to read; there are already enough anxious children in the homes where anxious parents have read these books. We do not want to add to the stresses suffered by many children because of well-intentioned but misguided parents.

We'd like to remove much of the anxiety that children and parents feel about reading by providing a number of purposeful, *pleasant* activities that will help your children to be ready to read *when that time comes*.

That's why the title of this book is *Ready to Read*. We want to help you prepare your children for a formal reading program that should be the responsibility of professional teachers. This book is not intended to be a step-by-step guide for teaching a pre-first-grade child to read. The primary role of parents in the reading process prior to first grade is to encourage their children's oral language, to help build their interest in the printed word, and to provide a wide background of experiences for their children in a natural and informal manner.

HOW DID YOUR PARENTS HELP YOU GET READY TO READ?

Think back to your own early childhood. Did your parents read to you at bedtime? Did they take time each day to talk to you or tell you stories? Did they take you to the library? Did they buy you books? Did you have books, magazines, or newspapers in your home? Did your parents encourage you to do well in school? Did they let you know that they loved you regardless of how well you did on your report card? Did they provide you with a place to study? Did they help you feel good about being the person you are?

Our parents are powerful role models for us. They are our first teachers. Some parents love to teach their children and are able to spend a lot of time doing it. In her autobiography, *Times to Remember*, Rose Kennedy tells of clipping articles from the daily newspaper and taping them to the wall near the dining room. As her children came to dinner, each child would pick up a clipping, read it, and prepare to tell the others at the dining table about it. This was one way the Kennedy children, while still young, became interested in current affairs and learned to talk with others about what they had read.

Bronson Alcott, a progressive American educator of the nineteenth century and the father of Louisa Mae Alcott, is said to have formed letters with his body and pieces of furniture. Alcott had his daughters imitate him, and so made the alphabet a very personal and fun part of their young lives.

As authors, we've looked back at what our parents did to help us get ready for reading. One of us can recall in great detail his pre-first-grade experiences with comic books. His father operated a magazine stand in East Texas, and when he was four and five years of age his father allowed him to take home comic books to "read." He remembers sitting up in bed "reading" his books while his mother and father read their newspapers and magazines.

The other author remembers storytelling by her father, who had been raised in Czechoslovakia. Before bedtime, she would crawl up onto her father's lap to hear another exciting story that he had been told as a child. It was a favorite part of her day. It was not until she was in school that she learned that all her father's stories came from a book entitled *Aesop's Fables*.

Perhaps you can remember a childhood experience which caused you to become interested in reading. It's important to remember that our parents and your parents did what they did without any help from "experts." The role of parents was little studied until recently. Today, however, there is a growing understanding of the role parents play in the reading process and the positive effects it can have in the lives of young readers.

THE IMPORTANCE OF PARENTS IN EARLY LEARNING

In a 1976 issue of *Childhood Education*, Nancy Larrick, one of the first to recognize the importance of parents in the reading process, wrote:

> The role of parents as home teachers was not generally understood twenty years ago. Research studies in the past decade have focused attention on the tremendous growth potential of young children. Given the opportunity, they may reach out to more advanced concepts, more mature language patterns, and greater understanding than many adults have thought possible. Furthermore, there seems to be evidence that the intellectual development in a child's early years will

strongly influence his potential for development as a teenager and adult.

Six years later, the International Reading Association (IRA) stated that "the quality of home and community experiences during the early years is crucial for children's future educational success." Educators now have ample evidence that parents can play a very significant role in preparing their children for formal reading programs. Among the recent findings reviewed by the IRA are these:

1. Many children probably gain a somewhat greater amount of functional knowledge from their homes and communities than they do from their schools.
2. Good readers come from homes that are psychologically comfortable, that foster positive attitudes toward reading and learning, and that provide stimulating cultural and language experiences.
3. Parents who are encouraged or are trained to do so can be effective in providing cultural experiences and many simple learning experiences.
4. Brothers, sisters, aunts, uncles, and grandparents can make valuable contributions through informal tutoring.

Prior to the 1950s, the parents' role in the learning process was not heavily emphasized by professional educators. Today parents are encouraged to take an active role in children's language development. What parents may have done incidentally in the past is now recognized as very important to the early development of children.

WHAT IS READING?

If you were asked what reading is, what would you say? Is reading identifying letters that have been grouped into words? Is it getting meaning out of a sentence or a paragraph? Is it calling out words properly when you see them? Is it bringing meaning to words based on your own previous experiences? Reading is all these things, and more.

No single definition of reading is completely satisfactory. Reading is an integral part of human communication, a complex process which begins during infancy and includes talking, listening, and writing as well as reading. Reading involves the recognition and interpretation of what is read in the light of personal experience; children must get meaning from what they read, or they have done nothing but pronounce words. Readiness for reading begins to develop during infancy. Children learn about the importance of reading as they watch parents and siblings read such everyday items as cereal boxes, letters, road signs, and billboards. They soon learn that people get information from symbols presented in written or printed form. The seed of reading readiness has been planted.

WHAT IS READING READINESS?

Although the term "reading readiness" was introduced over half a century ago, its definition continues to change. Today there are three prevalent viewpoints concerning reading readiness:

1. Some educators view reading readiness as a continuing process which begins when a child learns a language and ends with adult reading skills. Learning to read, in this view, is like learning to ride a skateboard or to play squash. One must begin with easy steps and progress until one is proficient.
2. Other educators regard reading readiness as a specific phase in a child's development. These educators view a child's maturity (physical, emotional, experiential, intellectual, and social) as the most important factor in the ability to learn to read.
3. Some educators see reading readiness as a sequence of activities planned to get a child ready to move into a formal reading program. In theory, once a child has mastered certain specific skills, usually taught in a prescribed sequence, he or she is ready to move into a formal reading program.

Most educators, however, agree that reading readiness includes the following components:

1. *Oral language*: that is, the ability to understand language, and an understanding of how speech becomes print.
2. *Listening*: the ability to follow directions and recall events.

3. *Experiential background*: as shown by the ability to recall experiences prior to school and share them with others.
4. *Auditory discrimination*: the ability to note likenesses and differences in the sounds of words, such as whether they rhyme, begin or end with the same sound, or have similar middle sounds.
5. *Visual discrimination*: an understanding that pictures, letters, and words either look alike or are different.
6. *Eye-hand coordination* or *perceptual-motor skills*: the ability to recognize that one reads print from left to right, and well-developed motor control, as shown by the ability to draw, trace, copy, and write on the line.
7. *Interest*: showing an interest in books and seeking them out to look at, handle, or take home.

CHILDREN AND PARENTS ARE NOT ALL ALIKE

The study of children reveals many important differences among them. You've probably already noticed this in your own home if you have more than one child. Even children with the same parents and the same home environment have different abilities, interests, and learning styles.

Since each child is unique, you should not compare children with each other, expecting them to behave and learn in exactly the same way. Although we refer throughout this book to some of the general characteristics of children at each stage of development, these are only general guides and not a precise description of any child's behavior at that stage. If your child appears to be especially "fast" or "slow" during the early years, this is no cause for either elation or concern. Your child is merely revealing his or her unique pattern of development. If you have any special worries, however, by all means check with your family doctor, pediatrician, or public health agency. It's always better to get answers to your questions than to worry about them.

Parents, too, are not all alike. And today many different people play parental roles, at least temporarily: grandparents, baby-sitters, and older siblings, as well as others in the neighborhood. The ideas in this book are appropriate for anyone living with and caring for children.

We also realize that not every child has two and only two

parents; not every child has even one parent for most of the day. In suggesting activities throughout the book, we've considered different family situations and provided ways of adapting the activity if necessary. We've also tried not to focus only on mothers. Fathers have an important role to play in the development of their children. This is so even if they are only weekend fathers, as in many families today.

Our goal in this book is to encourage you to play a more active role in helping your child to read by providing information and suggested activities that will help you and your child during the preschool and primary-grade years. The activities that follow should help you to become a partner with your child's teachers in the exciting venture of helping your child become an effective and enthusiastic reader.

2

ACTIVITIES FOR THE INFANT AND TODDLER
(BIRTH THROUGH AGE TWO)

When you bring your baby home from the hospital, he or she enters a learning environment for which you are responsible. The home is the first educational institution, and you are your child's first teacher.

From the earliest years of your child's life, you will be providing experiences that will be useful later, when he or she starts a formal reading program. In this chapter, we'll describe the common characteristics of children of this age as they begin to develop their communication skills, and we'll suggest activities that you and your child will enjoy and learn from.

HOW AN INFANT COMMUNICATES

From birth until one year, your child communicates in many ways: crying, smiling, and babbling; making sounds that show comfort or discomfort; vocalizing (instead of crying) when alone; looking toward a source of sound; vocalizing syllables, such as *ba, da,* and *ka;* combining syllables such as *da-da, ba-ba,* and *ma-ma;* and responding to voices with eye contact or a smile, or by turning toward the speaker.

While still an infant, your baby learns to wave *bye-bye* and play patty-cake. He or she looks around when asked, "Where is kitty?" (or mommy or daddy). Your baby jabbers expressively, imitates animal sounds, and enjoys listening to conversation, music, and singing. The child learns to stop when told "No-no," and with encouragement may have learned words besides "Mama" and "Dada."

HOW A ONE-YEAR-OLD COMMUNICATES

During the next year of development, your son or daughter will be listening intently to adults and others nearby. There will be signs of an increased interest in and knowledge of words. Your one-year-old may be able to point to familiar people, body parts, animals, toys, or pictures in a book, as well as to point to and request objects such as milk, cookies, or a toy. A one-year-old often begins to say more words, or tries to combine jargon ("baby talk") and words to carry on a conversation alone or with others. He or she usually can follow simple commands, understand simple questions, and echo words when asked. Many one-year-olds are interested in looking at pictures for two or more minutes if they are named by an adult or an older brother or sister.

As the child approaches eighteen months, he or she shows a more pronounced growth of learning. He or she learns more body parts and can point to them on request. Most eighteen-month-olds can name three or four pictures of common objects, and they can ask for food or water when hungry or thirsty. They can refer to themselves by name, say or respond to approximately twenty words, and even try to use pronouns ("me," "you," "it").

HOW A TWO-YEAR-OLD COMMUNICATES

The third year of life is often referred to as the "terrible twos." Life with a two-year-old isn't always hectic, but most two-year-olds are expanding their environments by walking and getting into more things than a parent would want them to. Your two-year-old will begin to speak grammatically, using three-word sentences. The typical two-year-old may be able to say about fifty words. Most two-year-olds can name common objects and can choose one object from a group of objects when asked. Your two-year-old can probably point to the ear or another body part when asked a question such as "What do you hear with?" He or she names *one* color correctly, joins in singing or saying parts of nursery rhymes or songs, and begins to use plurals correctly.

At about twenty-five to twenty-six months, the toddler can follow a two-stage direction, such as "Get the book and close the door." He or she can tell or show the use of common objects, understands most adjectives, and shows an interest in explanations of "why" and "how." As the toddler reaches two and one-half years of age or older, he or she can point to and repeat the names of six body parts, ask spontaneous questions, speak two hundred or more recognizable words, and give his or her name on request. Two-and-a-half-year-olds regularly relate experiences from the past and use several verb forms and tenses correctly.

YOUR CHILD'S EARLIEST LANGUAGE DEVELOPMENT

Some adults have the misconception that an infant's first nine months of life are a time of lots of sleeping and little learning. Quite the contrary! Approximately a day after birth, a child begins to observe and learn about the world. Infants begin to observe the faces of those who attend to their needs and learn to respond with a smile, coo, or gurgle. From birth, infants are curious about their outside world.

Listening is an infant's major means of learning. Infants at birth respond to sounds they hear. They quickly learn to pay attention to sounds that are important to them: the footsteps and voices of family members; the opening and closing of the refrigerator door; their name spoken during feeding, changing, dressing, and at other times. Through listening, infants learn to recognize familiar voices of family members and others.

Since infants are eager to learn more about their environment, they listen to speech and gradually learn to associate meanings with the words they hear. Radio, TV, conversations of adults and other children, stories and poems read aloud, and explanations to questions all give the infant experience in listening. Since infants have a short attention span, do not expect them to pay attention for a prolonged period of time. Instead, continue to play their records and music boxes and talk to them, and recognize that they will tune in and tune out of listening.

By twelve to fourteen months, most children understand such words as these:

hi	kitty (cat)
dog (doggy)	cup
cracker	car
eyes	ears
feet	hair
come here	sit down
stand up	stop that
hug	water
drink	chair (highchair)
book	socks
patty-cake	peek a boo
kiss	bring
brush your hair	kiss me
get up	

(Burton L. White, *The First Three Years of Life*. Englewood Cliffs, N.J.: Prentice-Hall, 1975, p. 84. Reprinted by permission.)

As infants grow, they learn to associate listening with talking as parts of the communication process. Infants first emit sounds to indicate comfort and discomfort; then, by experimenting with sounds, they become aware that sounds can be controlled. Your responses encourage them to make particular sounds, and the result is the first *intentional* vocalizing, as the infant learns to say "Mama," "Dada," or "Wawa" for *Mommy, Daddy,* and *water.*

Generally speaking, an eight-month-old infant begins to speak in one-word sentences that depend upon nonverbal cues and context. Then two-word sentences, such as "Dada gone," emerge. As the infant's knowledge increases, more meaning is conveyed through words. Many two-year-olds listen intently and carry on real conversations with other children and adults.

It's important to realize that children vary in the age they first produce words and in what first word they say. If there are older siblings or if the child has no need to talk because a parent anticipates the infant's every wish, the child may be eighteen to twenty-four months old before words are produced. If so, be sure to note whether the infant can understand spoken words. For example, if you asked the child to do something such as hand you a ball, does he or she do it? If so, the possibility of deafness is ruled out.

Don't be discouraged if your child is not talking by twelve months of age. Each child learns and develops at an individual rate. "The past twenty years," a group of well-known experts on child development has written, "have been devoted to efforts to improve or speed up infant behavior. However, so far no one has demonstrated that we can speed up any behavior substantially by things we do for and with the infant or child." (Gesell et al., *Infant and Child in the Culture of Today.* New York: Harper & Row, 1972.)

TALKING WITH AND LISTENING TO YOUR CHILD

Parents of infants and toddlers have many opportunities to talk with and listen to their children. Talking allows the infant to identify the voices of parents and other caretakers and to form associations between sounds and actions.

Have you ever heard an adult talk to an infant while changing the child's diaper? For example, "My, what is all this fuss about? Are you wet?" (changes diaper). "There, Chris, you're dry again. Is that better? Of course it is!"

The infant doesn't know what was said but may respond with a smile, or an "ah" or "oo."

Have you ever fed a baby a bottle of water, juice, or milk? While giving the bottle, you probably made some remark like, "Here's something to fill your tummy." Or perhaps you recall trying to convince a child to eat some peas and beef and strained pears. Of course, the beef and pears were acceptable, but the peas were rejected! Perhaps you used the old airplane trick: "Michael, let's pretend you're an airplane and this spoonful of food is a passenger." Meanwhile, you shoved the spoonful of peas and beef into his mouth. Hopefully, it wasn't ejected.

One of the authors has many friends with young children and enjoys spending time with the children. At one household, the routine is for a guest to walk into the room, greet everyone individually, drink a cup of coffee, survey the new toys, and watch how each one works. Finally, a book is pulled out and a toddler says, "Please read!" The adult reads the story, and everyone is content. Once this half-hour routine is completed, the children go off to play with each other, stopping to check if the adults are around. From time to time the adults take the time to see what is happening and occasionally end up eating "pretend" meals or taking a "pretend" ride in the wagon. This time is enjoyable for the visitor as well as the children. It provides the visitor a chance to catch up with what is new in the lives of the children, to carry on the tradition of reading a story, and to have the children warm up to the visitor. It also provides the parents with a chance to visit with a friend and share the children's adventures.

All of these situations provide excellent opportunities to talk with and listen to your children. If talking with and listening to your infant or toddler do not come naturally to you, you may want to make a conscious effort to learn how. Try engaging in some of the following suggested activities from the University of Washington guide for promoting language development. They're grouped by age.

1 to 3 months:

- Smile and talk softly in a pleasant voice while holding, touching, and handling your infant.

4 to 8 months:

- Engage in smiling eye-to-eye contact while talking to your infant.
- Talk in response to your baby's babbling sounds; echo the sounds he or she makes.
- Talk with your infant during handling, while feeding, bathing, dressing, diapering, during bedtime preparation, and while holding.
- While talking to your infant, hold in position so that he or she can see your face.
- Have your infant placed at eye level while talking to him or her.

9 to 12 months:

- Gain your child's attention when giving simple directions, such as "no-no," which the child is now able to understand.
- Accompany directions with gestures; for example, extend your hand when you are asking the child to give you an empty bottle or glass.
- Talk with your child during feeding, bathing, and playtimes.
- Produce sounds that your child can reproduce, such as lip smacking and tongue clicking.
- Repeat directions frequently and have your child participate in the action: for example, "open and close the drawer," or "move your arms and legs up and down."
- Have your child respond to verbal directions: stand up, sit down, close door, open door, turn around, come here.

13 to 18 months:

- While feeding, name your baby's foods and eating utensils. Ask if he or she is enjoying the meal; review the day's events in a simple manner.
- Pronounce words while cooking and preparing foods.
- Identify toys when using them and explain their function.
- Encourage verbalization and expression of wants.

19 to 30 months:

- Continue to present concrete objects with words.
- Talk about activities your child is involved with.
- Include your child in conversations at mealtimes.
- Encourage speech by having your child express wants.
- Incorporate games into the bathing routine by having your child name and point to body parts.
- As your child gains confidence in remembering and using words, encourage less use of gestures.
- Count and name articles of clothing as you dress your child.
- Count and name silverware as it is placed on a table.
- Sort, match, and name glassware, laundry, cans, vegetables, and fruit with your child.
- Help your child develop a basic vocabulary to express safety needs and information about your neighborhood.

- Whenever possible, use a word, show the object, and have your child handle and use it. Encourage him or her to watch your face while you say the word and try to repeat it. *Don't exert too much pressure.*

31 to 36 months:
- Read stories with familiar content and with some detail: nonsense rhymes, humorous stories.
- Expect your child to follow simple commands.
- Give your child an opportunity to hear and repeat his or her full name.
- Listen to your child's explanations about pictures he or she draws.
- Encourage your child to repeat nursery rhymes alone and with others.
- Address your child by his or her first name.

(From Kathryn E. Bernard and Marcene L. Erickson, *Teaching Children with Developmental Problems: A Family Care Approach.* St. Louis: C. V. Mosby Co., 1976, pp. 83–86. Reprinted by permission.)

A useful technique in helping your children increase their vocabulary is to complete sentences for them. For example, if your child has noticed a McDonald's restaurant, you can say: "Yes, that is a McDonald's, where we sometimes stop for french fries and a soda." You may have already noticed that your child is beginning to ask many more questions, perhaps using two- or three-word phrases. For example, "Sandy gone" could mean "Where has Sandy gone?" By using your child's short sentence as the basis for an answer and extending it, you can give your child more information and help him or her to learn new words.

Here are some specific examples of how you can use this technique to extend your toddler's vocabulary:

Color words: red, blue, green, yellow, white, black, etc.
Child says: "That ball."
Your response: "That's a yellow ball."
Shape words: round, circle, square, triangle, etc.
Child says: "My box."
Your response: "Yes, you're holding your square box."
Label words: dog, cat, rose, book, truck, etc.
Child says: "Nice flower."
Your response: "This is a nice rose."
Class or family words: animal, food, toy, clothing, etc.
Child says: "Milk, bread, and soup."
Your response: "We need some food. Let's have soup, raisin bread, and some milk for lunch."
Material words: plastic, rubber, cotton, wood, etc.
Child says: "Red truck."
Your response: "Yes, you have a new red plastic truck."
Number words: One, two, three, etc.
Child says: "More blocks."
Your response: "Yes, there are many blocks. Let's count them. One, two, three."
Physical characteristics: size (big, small), texture (rough, smooth), density (solid, hollow, empty), method of construction (sewn together, pasted together), etc.
Child says: "Pretty coat."

Your response: "That's a nice new corduroy jacket. The pockets are sewn on the outside of the jacket."

You may not always remember to extend your child's sentences, nor should you always do it. Communication should be natural. It's just as important for you to learn to listen to your child and reinforce the words he or she uses correctly: "Yes, that's a book." "These are Jason's shoes." "Banana." "Sue is eating a banana." If your child mispronounces the word slightly, say it correctly; this encourages the child to experiment further with sounds and to try to say the word correctly. If your child uses "baby talk," recognize the words he or she is trying to pronounce, but do not talk in baby talk yourself. Through listening, your infant or toddler learns to understand and be understood. He or she also learns about how language works and how to communicate with others. With this experience, your child will learn to follow directions, to participate in social activities, such as sharing ideas with friends, and to understand the words in stories that are read aloud.

Parents of a toddler may want to prepare a list of words that their child knows for the baby-sitter or day-care worker. You might also want to ask the other adult to notice and jot down any new words your child learns.

READING TO YOUR CHILD

If you have a new baby, friends and family members may have bought your baby some gifts, such as a colorful bib, a blanket, a mobile, or perhaps a stuffed animal. You've hung the mobile, and your baby is having fun looking at the dangling objects. The bib and blanket have been put to use, and your baby appears to like the teddy bear. But why did your baby get a stiff book of Mother Goose rhymes from Uncle George, and a soft cloth number book from Aunt Sue? It will be years before your baby can read! Even though he or she won't understand what you are saying at first, reading to an infant is a good idea for several reasons. It introduces him or her to colorful pictures and pleasant sounds. An infant likes the experience of being held close and hearing his or her parent's voice nearby. Babies also enjoy looking at a picture book and hearing their parent name the objects on each page. It's a special time in the day that is different from any other parent-child activity.

So it's not true that picture books should be saved until your child is ready to read. Most children's picture books are actually written for reading aloud. There are wordless books that have pictures only, and easy-reading books designed for the beginning reader. However, many picture books have words and sentences that would be too difficult for the beginning reader to read alone. Even infants and toddlers, however, can enjoy the beautiful sounds and pictures that the authors and illustrators have created.

If your baby has not received a book as a baby gift and you need to economize, try looking for books at yard sales, bazaars, and thrift stores. Cloth or sturdy cardboard books are best for a child in the teething phase. If you are creative and want to make your own books, use file folders, the cardboard from the backs of tablets or shirts, or any other heavy material. Find simple, colorful pictures with only a few objects and glue them on the cardboard. For example, if you like pictures of horses, make a horse book showing the various breeds of horses. If you like cars, cut out pictures from car advertisements. Other pictures could be used for books about toys, musical instruments, pets, sea animals, barnyard animals, or other topics. To keep your book together, punch two holes along the left-hand side of the cardboard and attach the pages together with yarn, string, or an old shoelace. The book may only be four or five pages long, but it can provide your child with real enjoyment. Look at the pictures, talk about them, and even make up your own stories. Your book will be personalized and will survive abuse by little hands and curious mouths.

Of course, you can buy books for your child as well. Literally hundreds of new books are produced each year for young children, and selecting the best ones is a challenge. Many parents use their personal preference or the child's interests as a guide. Others prefer to follow lists provided by preschool teachers or the children's librarians in a public library. But remember: any list of books for children is only *a guide*, not a final word on what your child will like. Children vary in attitudes and interests. Therefore, consider your child's individuality when selecting books (and, for that matter, games, records, and toys as well).

Here are some reference books that can help you choose good books for your children:

Best Books for Children: Preschool Through the Middle Grades, 2nd ed., ed. by John T. Gillespie and Christine B. Gilbert. New York: R. R. Bowker Company, 1981.

Bibliography of Books for Children, 1980 ed. Washington, D.C.: Association for Childhood Education International.

Children & Books, 5th ed., by Zena Sutherland and May Hill Arbuthnot. Glenview, Ill.: Scott, Foresman & Company, 1976.

Children's Book Choices for 1982, produced yearly in October. Write to the International Reading Association, in Newark, Del., for a free reprint.

A Parent's Guide to Children's Reading, 4th ed., by Nancy Larrick. Garden City, N.Y.: Doubleday & Company, 1975.

Parents Magazine Baby Care Book by Eleanor S. Duncan, Mary E. Buchanan, and Dorothy V. Whipple. New York: Parents Magazine Enterprises, 1965.

Supertot by Jean Marzallo. New York: Harper & Row, 1979.

What Books and Records Should I Get for My Preschooler? by Norma Rogers. Newark, Del: International Reading Association, 1972.

The following is a list of books recommended by our local librarians for infants and toddlers:

Mother Goose

Mother Goose. *Book of Nursery and Mother Goose Rhymes*. Marguerite de Angeli, illustrator, Garden City, N.Y.: Doubleday, 1954.

Mother Goose. *A Collection of Nursery Rhymes*. Brian Wildsmith, illustrator. New York: Watts, 1965.

Mother Goose. *The Mother Goose Treasury*. Raymond Briggs, illustrator. New York. Coward, 1966.

Mother Goose. *Real Mother Goose*. Blanche F. Wright, illustrator. Chicago, Ill.: Rand McNally, 1944.

Mother Goose. *The Tall Book of Mother Goose*. Fedor Rojankovsky, illustrator. New York: Harper & Row, 1942.

Sleepy Time Books

Brown, Margaret Wise. *A Child's Good Night Book*. Reading, MA: Young Scott Books, 1950.

———. *Goodnight Moon*. New York: Harper & Brothers, 1947.

———. *The Runaway Bunny*. New York: Harper & Row, 1972.

Zolotow, Charlotte. *Sleepy Book*. New York: Lothrop, 1958.

Concept Books

Bruna, Dick. *b is for bear: an abc book*. New York: Methuen, 1972.

Garfinkel, Bernard Max. *Zoo Book: A Child's World of Animals*. New York: Platt & Munk, 1968.

Matthieson, Thomas. *Things to See: A Child's World of Familiar Objects*. New York: Platt & Munk, 1966.

Reiss, John. *Colors*. Scarsdale, N.Y.: Bradbury Press, 1969.

———. *Numbers*. Scarsdale, N.Y.: Bradbury Press, 1971.

Rojankovsky, Fedor. *Animals on the Farm*. New York: Knopf, 1967.

Spier, Peter. *Crash! Bang! Boom!*. Garden City, N.Y.: Doubleday, 1972.

Rhymes & Stories for the Very Young

Brooke, Leonard Leslie. *Johnny Crow's Garden*. New York: Warne, 1903.

Carle, Eric. *The Very Hungry Caterpillar*. New York: World Publisher, 1970.

Hutchins, Pat. *Happy Birthday Sam*. New York: Greenwillow, 1978.

———. *Titch*. New York: MacMillan, 1971.

Kraus, Robert. *Whose Mouse are You?* New York: MacMillan, 1970.

Langstaff, John M. *Over in the Meadow*. New York: Harcourt, Brace & Jovanovich, 1967.
Lionni, Leo. *Inch by Inch*. Stamford, CT: Astor-Honor, 1960.
Nakatani, Chiyoko. *My Teddy Bear*. New York: Crowell, 1976.
Williams, Garth. *The Chicken Book: A Traditional Rhyme*. New York: Delacorte 1970.

The Children's Book Council recommends that you keep these basic points in mind when selecting a book for an infant or a preschool child:

1. Young children are attracted by brightly colored pictures of simple objects.
2. They will listen attentively if a book with a simple text and a lively rhythm is selected for them.
3. They are visually and mentally stimulated by wordless books that encourage them to create their own stories.
4. They are delighted with heavy cardboard books or cloth books, which have the virtue of being practically indestructible.

Besides considering the *what* of reading to children, parents should also consider *when*. Nancy Larrick says: "Many parents plan a regular time for reading aloud each day. Just before bedtime is a traditional choice; whatever the hour, be sure to make it the same time each day so the child will look forward to it as he does to lunch or supper."

If you do not have much free time and can't read to your child every day, try to spend a few minutes a week reading to him or her. If your child doesn't like to be cuddled while being read to, then place him or her in the crib and sit nearby as you read a few pages of a story.

As your child approaches age one, you will notice that he or she likes to tell you the names of familiar objects on a page when being read to. Take the time to ask your child questions, such as "Can you find the dog on this page?" or "Where is the boy going—to the bus or to the park?" Wait for your child to point to the answer *or* give you a short response. If the answer is correct, praise your child. If the answer is wrong, give the correct answer: "No, that's not a lamb, it's a pig. Here is the lamb" (point to the correct animal). As the child listens to more stories, introduce new objects and characters on the pages. Your child will begin recognizing more in the future.

By this time you can enjoy sharing your favorite picture books, nursery rhymes, and stories with your child.

BEING A READING MODEL FOR YOUR CHILD

Showing your child that you read and value reading will set a good example for him or her. Raising a family takes a lot of time, and with the demands of work, shopping, cooking, and so on, there may not be much free time for pleasure reading. On the other hand, you probably still read the mail, magazine articles, newspapers, comics, and so on. Reading in front of your child will help him or her to understand that you value reading.

Think of all the things you read in a week. Here's a partial list:

advertisements	manuals
billboards	maps
brochures	menus
bumper stickers	phone book
catalogs	posters
the dictionary	recipes
directories in	shopping bags
buildings and	tickets
elevators	want ads
door signs	weather reports
greeting cards	on TV
labels on clothing,	
cans, and jars	

Every time your child sees you gathering useful information in this way, he or she is gaining a valuable lesson in the importance of reading.

Children are great imitators, as you'll realize when you see your toddler trying to read a book to a doll or pet.

INVOLVING YOUR CHILD IN A VARIETY OF RECREATIONAL ACTIVITIES

Adults usually marvel at the fragility of tiny infants under six weeks of age: "Oh, look how tiny and delicate the hands are." It is understandable that parents and other adults sometimes feel nervous about holding an infant, let alone playing with

one. But as the infant approaches four months of age, becomes stronger, and is more mobile, adults try more activities.
Did you ever see the expressions on the faces of an infant and
a parent as they made faces at one another? The smile, the
frown, and the surprised look are fascinating to watch.

One of the fun things about being a parent is having the
opportunity to pass on to your child some of the games that
are part of your family heritage. The games that you first play
with your child will most likely be those that your parents
played with you, games such as "Peekaboo," "Patty-Cake,"
and "This Little Piggy Went to Market." If you talk to your
infant as you play these games, your child will begin to see
how you enjoy words through your facial expressions and
tone of voice. Playing games with your child involves you in a
way that is a bit different from what you normally do. It helps
your child to see your playful side rather than you only as a
caretaker. Games also introduce infants to the sounds of
words and to relationships among words, such as in their
rhythm and rhyme.

Young children need stimulation and are eager to learn
about the world about them. Their toys can include many
objects that are inexpensive or can be made at home by
parents and grandparents—for example, toys made from
cloth, such as rag dolls, stocking dolls, or animals, or from
wood, such as simple building blocks. You can easily turn
trash to treasure with the help of a little ingenuity and work.
Use common sense and safety precautions when making toys
for young children. For example, young infants and toddlers
often put things into their mouths. Therefore, do not use
small, loose objects as toys, and never use toxic paints, glues,
or finishes.

Infants from birth to nine months typically enjoy listening
to, watching, or playing with music boxes, mobiles, crib toys,
animals on a string, cradle gyms, teething rings, large beads
and blocks, rattles, and cuddly toys. Infants nine months to a
year and half seem to like balls, rag dolls, floating toys for the
bathtub, stacking toys (such as stacking rings), push and pull
toys (such as telephones), jacks-in-the-box, snap-lock beads,
and small pushing or riding toys.

Toddlers age eighteen months to two years like sandboxes;

peg and mallet toys; wading pools; swings; bean-bag toys; toys for digging, pushing, and pulling; play dollhouses with people; barn and farm animals; dump trucks and other trucks with movable parts; big wooden beads that can be strung, stacked, or dropped into containers; shape toys; and modeling dough. Some of these toys can be made with materials found at home. For example, wooden spools come in a variety of sizes and colors; get family and friends to save them for you. Long shoelaces can be used to string the spools and beads.

The two-to-three-year-old toddler enjoys imitating adults, so plastic or metal toy dishes, utensils, and kitchen supplies are useful as toys. They also like inflatable balls; large cast-metal or wooden trucks, planes, trains, or workbenches; simple musical toys such as a cymbal, drum, or chime; simple puzzles (six to eight pieces) made of wood or heavy card-board; tricycles, wagons, or wheelbarrows; bubble-blowing liquid; playground equipment, such as slides; and baby dolls and doll accessories.

When making or purchasing toys, consider durability and simplicity. For example, when children first learn to manipulate a block and put it in a hole, they need only a few pieces; so too with a puzzle. Choose or select a puzzle that will require the child to put a shape or a few shapes into their proper places; then advance to puzzles with six to eight pieces. Of course, not all toddlers learn to put puzzles together rapidly, but if your child proves adept, then get ones with more pieces. The same is true with other kinds of toys. Simple toys are best.

Another way of having fun with your child is to enjoy sounds together. An infant responds to the voice of his or her mother or father before recognizing faces. Long before real speech, the child vocalizes for the pure pleasure of trying out sounds. The pleasure that comes from hearing different sounds is part of the infant's world.

You can add to the child's enjoyment of sounds through the use of soothing records, music boxes, and musical crib toys. You may also want to sing some of your favorite songs and lullabies, mentioning your child's name when appropriate.

Exposure to a variety of rhythms and types of music enables the infant or toddler to respond to a variety of moods. Soft music can lull your child to sleep, while marches featuring drums and trumpets will cause the child to be more alert and respond with body movements.

As children get older, they may have favorite songs. They like to dance to these songs, trying to imitate the dance movements they have seen adults make. Children often respond differently to the variety of songs on a record or on TV or radio, by marching, hopping, or swaying. Folk tunes, marches, and nursery rhymes are especially popular with toddlers.

You may also wonder if your interest in art will be of value to your infant or toddler. The answer is yes. Art is part of the life of your child from the earliest days at home. Think about the colors he or she sees in the rooms of the apartment or house. You introduce your child to the world of colors, designs, and textures through the selection of your home furnishings, your clothes, and the toys you select for your child. These early sensory experiences with the basic elements of art establish a foundation on which your child will draw throughout life.

Babies need and enjoy visual stimulation because one of their earliest developmental tasks is to create pictures in their minds of the things around them. As they get older, however, they also need to act on their environment. Although all children are messy at times, they need to be able to splash soapsuds during their bath, to rip up old newspapers and magazines, to play with foods such as oatmeal by smearing them on tabletops, highchairs, or trays, to drop objects over the sides of their cribs or playpens, and to do other "creative" things which allow them to see immediately the results of various behaviors. Such activities help them understand that they can influence their environment on their own and will serve as a foundation for their communicating their ideas through art when they are older.

You can provide your toddler with large sheets of paper and crayons as he or she begins to show a greater interest in art. But don't expect a young artist to emerge immediately! According to those who have carefully studied the behavior of children below the age of two, most of their attempts to express themselves through art are "exploratory"—that is, they are just trying to find out what their bodies will do and what can be done with the art materials. When they play with clay, they are not usually trying to represent anything specific, and when they scribble with crayon or pencil, they are not usually trying to communicate anything in particular. The *process* is much more important to the child than the *product*. So don't ask your children to tell you about their scribbles or to label them, because they're usually not interested in that. Right now, children just want the experience of making all those beautiful colors on a page. Later they will begin to generate and record ideas so that their parents and others can know about their feelings and experiences.

All of these early attempts at artistic expression will become important as children become interested in the printed word and the experiences they can share through reading. A drawing is often a child's first means of communicating an experience and thus is a step toward the use of written language in communication.

What is the value of television in the life of an infant or toddler? Much has been written about the negative and positive effects of television. Those who would advise you not to allow your child to watch TV believe that TV causes children to become passive adults. Some antitelevision writers have even referred to TV as the "plug-in drug." Some critics of TV believe that the programs, especially on commercial television, are too violent and promote antisocial behavior in children. Many critics also think TV is bad for children because of the commercials. Many children will see a shabby toy or a sugar-coated cereal advertised on TV and then beg their parents for it.

Those who believe that television can be beneficial, if used wisely, recommend it as an additional way for children to learn about their world. TV is an opportunity for children to learn about the varied types of people who live in our society and around the world.

We agree with this second viewpoint. Your child will have the opportunity, through television, to see people, places, and things that you could never expose him to in person. It's important, however, to be selective in choosing TV shows for your children and to talk with your child about the shows he or she watches. If TV is used as a baby-sitter, the child is left with the impression that it is okay to sit for hours in front of the television, ignoring the many other things that can be done with leisure time.

Study the TV listings and the reviews in your newspaper to get a better idea of the content of programs, and ask your child some questions about what he or she knows of the topics treated. Many good children's programs allow the child to participate by responding to questions or doing something during or after the program. After a child has seen something on television which interests him or her, you may want to find picture books at the library related to that topic.

GOING PLACES WITH YOUR CHILD

Today there are many different types of baby-carriers for use in a car or on a parent's body. Such carriers help to keep infants safe and parents comfortable as well. Because of this, babies go practically everywhere today. Some mothers or fathers even take them to work in an emergency. Today's well-traveled infants are soaking up new sights and sounds as they share the places that their parent is experiencing.

Take your baby with you to the grocery store, the drugstore, the shopping center, the health-food store, and the other places you go during a busy day. Take your baby to the playground, and while pushing the swing, talk about what you did on your way to the playground, about the things that can be seen from the swing, or about what you will do as you head homeward.

The zoo, an amusement park, a lake, a circus, a plant nursery, a pet show, or an arts and crafts fair are also enjoyable for infants. Your child will have a broader background of experiences with which to compare sights and sounds. For instance, at the zoo you and your child saw some animals roaming free in a large habitat, while others sat in cages; however, at the pet show the dogs and cats had no cages. Compare the sounds you heard at the circus with those you heard at the lake: How were they alike? How were they different? Point out some of the likenesses and differences to your child.

Your child is eager to explore the environment. This is a very natural part of the behavior of a healthy child. There is no reason to limit your trips to places that seem appropriate for the young child. Do things you enjoy doing, and take the child along. Your son or daughter will learn new vocabulary, develop new concepts, and learn about new situations that will help him or her to understand new ideas.

OUTSIDE CHILD CARE FOR INFANTS AND TODDLERS

Since education is a lifelong process that begins with birth and continues until death, there are programs for infants and toddlers that have educational benefits related to reading. This does not mean that the young prenursery-school child is being taught to read in any formal sense, nor that programs should focus only on the intellectual development of the child. It does mean that children are constantly learning and that good programs for infants and toddlers take this fact into consideration.

Since World War II, American families have undergone many changes. Instead of the traditional nonworking mother and working father, we have many working parents, and single parents who are primarily weekend parents. As a result, many children are being placed in day-care centers or child-care centers during their infancy and toddler years. These centers can be publicly or privately operated. If you are investigating day-care centers for your child, local city or county human welfare departments or social service offices can give you suggestions regarding the public centers. You can also write for information to these two groups:

Day Care and Child Development Council of America, Inc.
1401 K Street, N.W.
Washington, D.C. 20005

Child Welfare League of America, Inc.
44 East 23rd Street
New York, N.Y. 10010

Day-care or child-care services fall under several headings: family day care, institutional (group) day care, and nursery school.

Family day-care programs for infants and toddlers are usually run by women within their own homes. Although the standards for the training of teachers and the cleanliness of the environment vary from state to state, many teachers in family day-care programs are licensed to take care of young children in their homes and have had training for this responsibility.

Institutional or group day care provides services for children in a setting outside a home. Again, the regulations related to the training of the teachers and the environment vary, but if you search carefully, you will probably find a program that suits your needs and the needs of your child.

The term "nursery school" typically describes a school for children ages two and a half through four with an educational program. Typically there is a qualified teacher, trained in early childhood education, to teach the children on a half-day or full-day basis. (See Chapter 3 for further information on nursery-school programs.)

3

ACTIVITIES FOR THE
NURSERY-SCHOOL-AGE CHILD
AGES THREE AND FOUR

Living with a nursery-school-age child is indeed an adventure! Three- and four-year-olds are assertive, adventurous, and demanding. They want to do things for themselves, discover new things, and communicate their ideas. The three-year-old has become a real person who has learned to talk and communicate with adults and other children. The three-year-old can also feed and dress himself or herself, share toys with others, and take turns when playing games. Most can understand simple explanations, recite some rhymes, follow directions, pick up after themselves, and carry a simple tune. They enjoy building things, taking them apart, and imitating adults.

The four-year-old is even more competent than the three-year-old. You may be amazed at the words some four-year-olds know: "Grandpa used his lawn mower and his leaf mulcher on Saturday." Four-year-olds are toilet-trained and can wash their own hands and faces with ease. They can count objects in a picture book, can recognize a few letters of the alphabet, and may print one or more recognizable letters or numbers. They enjoy playing with other children and may seek the companionship of favorite playmates.

During this stage, play becomes the major "work" of the child. It's difficult for adults to appreciate fully the importance of play in the life of a young child. In our lives, work and play are generally completely separate. Very few of us consider our work as enjoyable as our play. For young children, however, play *is* work. Through play, they are able to face some of the same types of challenges and frustrations that we face in our work. They are able to test their bodies and their minds through play. Their play experiences are significant because through them children learn about themselves and their world in a way that is natural and appropriate for them.

Nursery-school-age children can fool adults by seeming very grownup one minute and very babyish the next. Sometimes they will speak in complete sentences and carry on an interesting conversation, and then, without warning, resort to baby talk or silly talk. They will play a game cooperatively and peacefully for a time, and then suddenly have difficulty behaving, coping, and cooperating with the other children. This changeability is a normal aspect of a child's growth.

TALKING WITH AND LISTENING TO YOUR CHILD

Although you may feel that your three- or four-year-old child talks too much, you should still reinforce his or her language skills by providing a broad background of experiences. You can do this simply by communicating with your child in the course of your daily routine. For instance, a mother may tell her child, "Cynthia, for lunch let's stop at the restaurant for a hot dog and french fries." Of course, if Cynthia likes this type of food for lunch, she'll say, "Yes! I'm hungry." Weeks later, Cynthia may be out with her grandfather when he says, "Cynthia, I'm hungry. I think I'd like a frankfurter and a milk shake. Would you like some lunch?" Cynthia nods, and they go off to eat lunch. Notice that Cynthia knew what food each adult was talking about, whether it was called a "hot dog" or a "frankfurter." This knowledge of more than one name for an object will aid her as she listens to stories and visualizes the meal a character in a book is having. She may use only the term "hot dog" in her conversation, but she knows another name for the same object. Her vocabulary has been enriched by a varied life and by the habit of using words to describe that life.

Here are some practical suggestions that can help you increase your three- or four-year-old's verbal skills:

1. One way to encourage a nursery-school-age child to talk is to provide some time with playmates. You might want to form a special group for this purpose. Several adults with their children can get together for two hours once a week

at a park or other enjoyable place. Play, including play with others, is important work for your child.

2. Take time to talk with your child about what he or she has done during the day. This is especially helpful if your child attends a day-care center or a nursery school. Show your child that you are interested in what he or she is doing. You'll be reinforcing the efforts of the nursery-school teacher as he or she provides ways for children to stimulate their verbal skills. You'll also give your child practice in communicating ideas and thoughts and help him or her to build a vocabulary.

3. Encourage your child to listen to you. Tell stories about experiences you had as a child. Tell about places you've visited, like the time you went to a dairy farm or the time you rode on an inclined cable car. You can even talk about the "good old days." Children like sharing their parents' experiences in this way.

4. Provide your child with toys and stuffed animals. Your child will love to play with and talk to the toys. A child doesn't always need a responsive audience when he or she chatters; sometimes the passive acceptance of a teddy bear or doll is even better than a lot of backtalk from an adult.

5. Toy telephones and tape recorders also help children develop their language skills. The child can talk for hours on the telephone. A tape recorder can be used in two ways. One way is to let your child listen to tapes of stories that accompany story books. Another way is to let your child tape-record a message that can be mailed to family or friends. We know of a family that has used the tape recorder effectively with a four-year-old boy. Once a month, his grandmother reads a story on one side of a tape cassette and then tapes a message on the second side. The child receives the tape, listens to it, and records a message for Grandmother. Then the grandmother makes up a new adventure, and the story continues.

6. Answer your child's questions. Give answers that are both honest and simple enough for a small child to grasp and understand. If a four-year-old asks, "What are twins?" you can answer, "Twins are two children who have the same birthday. Some twins look alike, and some do not look

alike." It is not necessary to give the genetic explanations. If the child asks, "How does the train work?" you can answer simply, "It runs by battery" or "It runs by electricity." Don't give the theory behind the principle. Most nursery-school-age children only want an answer to the question they have asked, not a lecture!

7. Introduce *opposites*, terms that show *relationships*, and *contractions* to your nursery-school-age child. Nursery-school-age children enjoy learning new terms such as *sad-happy, small-big, on-off,* and *hot-cold* (all pairs of opposites); *same-different, more-less, over-under, before-after, inside-outside,* and *beginning-end* (all terms that show relationships); and contractions, such as *don't* and *can't.* These are terms that will help your child to understand position and negatives in everyday language.

8. If your child is curious about letters and words, show how letters make words by using the magnetic letters you can buy in many toy stores or department stores. You can make simple words, such as color words (*red, blue*), body-part words (*arm, leg, head*), size and shape words (*big, round, flat*) and household-item words (*milk, table, chair, dish, cup*). We know of several parents who keep magnetic letters on the side of the refrigerator as a handy storage place. One mother keeps her shopping list up to date with magnetic letters. This delights her child.

9. Continue to encourage your child to listen to sounds, and from time to time ask him or her to tell you what sounds animals make. Your child may recall these sounds from any of a variety of sources—a trip to the zoo, a special TV program, a record, or a toy. Regardless of the source, he or she will be sharing sounds with you. You can ask even more questions to encourage your child to tell a story.

Occasionally children tend to chatter more than any one person has the time, patience, and energy to listen to. At times you will have to tell your child that you are too busy or too tired to listen. However, don't imply that you never want to hear him or her talk. Perhaps you may need to evaluate your own speaking and listening skills. Do you really like to talk, or are you a person of "few words"? Do you like to listen to others, or are you the kind of person who can't be bothered to hear other people out? As a parent, you may need the help of others— friends, relatives, grandparents, teachers, or other caretakers—to help your child develop his or her listening and speaking abilities.

READING TO YOUR CHILD

Nursery-school-age children tend to pay more attention when being read to than toddlers. Nursery-school-age children learn that the pages turn from right to left and that each page is read from left to right and from top to bottom. As they hear about the adventures of the characters in the stories, they expand their listening vocabulary.

As you read, you can gradually draw your child's attention to story sequences. Read to a certain point in a story and stop long enough to ask a question: "What do you think will happen next?" Listen to the answer, and then continue the story to see if it was correct. Later, you may want to ask your child to tell you highlights of the story while you are waiting in a supermarket or gasoline-station line. Does he or she have the correct story sequence? It's not crucial at this age, but understanding the sequence in a story is something to work toward. You can also use the sequencing skill at bedtime when discussing the activities the two of you did during the course of an afternoon or day.

Some nursery-school-age children are not interested in sitting still long enough to listen to a story in an adult's lap. Playing a child's record to accompany the story is one way to keep such a child interested. Not all children enjoy sitting in an adult's lap and listening to stories. There may be several reasons: The reader's voice may be dull or unanimated; the child may not like sitting on someone's lap; the child may find it hard to concentrate; the book may be too complicated or sophisticated; or the child may just be going through a phase in which he or she is not interested in reading.

Since nursery-school-age children enjoy silly talk, it's a natural time to introduce humorous books and those based on word play, such as *Amelia Bedelia* by Peggy Parrish and *The Day the King Rained* by Fred Gwynne. Listen with interest and encourage your child to express his or her ideas. Most libraries have a story hour for children. Take your child to these events from time to time. Don't give up reading to your child. Instead, try to find other books, such as books by Dr. Seuss, Mickey Mouse adventure stories, and so on. Whatever you do, don't compare your child with other brothers and sisters, relatives, friends' children, or even yourself. Many ABC books, such as *Zoophabets* by Robert Tallor, stimulate the learning of new words and the imagination of your child. There are several magazines, such as *Playmate*, designed for nursery-school-age children. The librarian can give you tips if you explain your child's interest.

James E. Flood, who has studied how parents help their children get ready to read, suggests these steps in reading aloud to children:

1. Start with warm-up questions; for example, you can ask your child, "Do you want to read this book?" or "Which book would you like to read?"
2. Let your child be part of the reading experience. Let him or her speak, ask and answer questions, and relate the content of the story to past experiences.
3. Be cheerful, encouraging, and positive as you read to your child.
4. Ask questions about the story after you finish reading it. This is good for your child because it completes the cycle of the reading experience and helps the child to understand the story completely.

If your child watches TV shows such as *Sesame Street* or *The Electric Company,* he or she may know some or all of the letters in the alphabet. You may want to use this knowledge by asking your child to point to words that begin with the known sounds. For example, three-and-a-half-year-old Michelle knows "M" and can point to the monkey and an "M" on any page of the Curious George series of books. However, she knows only a certain size of "M," and does not recognize it when the size of the letter is very large or very small. The more Michelle sees letters in various sizes of print, the more she will be able to recognize any "M."

We do not want to give you the impression that all children can be expected to master the alphabet by age four. However, some four-year-old children can say some letters of the alphabet, recognize them, or know the letters in their own names. Children learn about the alphabet through a variety of experiences, such as exposure to alphabet books, TV shows, records, and older brothers and sisters playing "school" with the younger child.

If your child seems interested in books but only likes to look at the pictures or count the items on a page, don't despair! Ask questions such as "How many ducks are on this page?" "What is the bird doing?" and "Where do you think the boy will go next?" This discussion and "pointing things out" in a picture during your reading time will help further your child's interest in learning to read. Some children just don't like long stories. Follow your child's cues! Look at the pictures, talk about them, and slowly ease into reading with one word or a single line of print on a page.

BEING A READING MODEL FOR YOUR CHILD

Some nursery-school-age children learn to read words and can recognize them in print. Researchers who have studied these early readers have found that they generally come from families that value language and reading. These children saw parents or siblings reading on a regular basis.

Listed below are some things you can read with your child to demonstrate the value of reading:

banners	greeting cards
book jackets	junk mail
cereal boxes	letters and notes
clocks	newspapers
clothing labels	phone books
comics and	posters
comic strips	restaurant menus
construction signs	riddles or puzzles
dictionaries	on place mats
directions on	TV listings
medicine bottles	

You may want to cook a meal and let your child help you by reading the recipe with you, even if you know it by heart. If you are shopping in a grocery store or department store, read the store directory to find the proper floor or aisle for the item you want to purchase. Young children enjoy being independent, so why not teach them how to read the signs and symbols on rest-room doors and water faucets as you do? One afternoon, while one of the authors was at the local branch of the public library, the following scene took place. A father with two young children left the reading room and headed toward the hall where the meeting rooms and rest rooms were located. He reminded his four-year-old daughter about looking at the doors, saying, "Which one do you go in?" She said, "The one with the *L* on it, because it stands for ladies." "What about washing your hands before you come out?" he continued. She replied, "*H* stands for hot and *C* stands for cold." Afterward, as she was getting her drink of water at the water fountain, one of the authors asked her, "What would you do if the rest rooms didn't say *Ladies* and *Gentlemen?* She replied, "I'd look for a *W,* 'cause it means *Women's Room!*" This child would have no trouble getting around in a library or a store, and she certainly benefited from seeing her father practicing his reading skills.

Perhaps you have some space where you can plant those flowers and vegetables that the family likes. Let your child see you reading the directions about planting and caring for those plants or vegetables. As the flowers and plants grow, read some gardening books about plant care with your child.

The point is that reading takes place all the time, even when it isn't recognized as reading. You are reading when you look through a phone directory, follow road signs and street signs, try to follow the directions to assemble a new bicycle together, or cook a frozen dinner.

GOING PLACES WITH YOUR CHILD

Three- and four-year-olds delight in seeing skits, puppet shows, short plays, or magic shows. Take advantage of your local community's schedule of events, such as the Fourth of July parade, the church bazaar, the drama club performance, and the community sing-along. Prepare your child for the event by talking about it beforehand. After watching the event, clear up any misconceptions your child may have.

From time to time, refer back to the event to encourage your child to recall sights, sounds, and experiences.

Contact your city, county, or state government, or check your local newspapers for your local calendar of events. In the Washington, D.C., area, for instance, there are tape-recorded messages about activities available by phone. Many other communities have similar services. There are also monthly newsletters available from many state and county offices which give you tips about things to do with your child. The Home and School Institute (Special Projects Office), 1707 H Street, N.W., Washington, DC 20006, provides information about regional programs and booklets for parental use.

You may have little free time to spend with your child or children. But no matter what your schedule or how busy you may be, take time to do things with your child. The times you share together will add to the background of your child's experiences. These trips or events will be stimulating for your child and will also enhance his or her speaking and listening vocabulary. Here are some illustrations of how this can happen. McKenzie was thirty-seven months old when she went to a miniature zoo in her hometown with her nursery-school class. There she saw a bear, along with a host of other animals. When she got home, all she could talk about was the bear she had seen at the zoo. Weeks later, when she returned to the zoo with her younger sister and her parents, McKenzie was able to recall many of the sights and sounds that she had heard. She even led the way to some of the animal cages! Another example: Christopher was thirty-nine months old when he was reminded of a picnic at a nearby lake while looking at a photo album. As he looked at the pictures, his dad talked about each picture, giving Christopher the opportunity to recall the event. As the afternoon passed in this pleasant reminiscence, Christopher decided he'd like to go to the lake again. This time he decided to invite some family friends in addition to his immediate family. Have you ever heard a child plan a future get-together? What enthusiasm and imagination the three- or four-year-old has!

You may not have the time or energy to come up with new ideas, but continue to do some of the things you did while your child was a toddler. For example, continue to spend time at a playground or park. Now that your child is older, you may notice that he or she will try the merry-go-round, the jungle gym, and the slides without much encouragement on your part. The repetition of trips to places you have visited before will not bore your child, since children's interests change continually. In fact, your child will probably notice and enjoy new things that he or she did not see on previous visits.

INVOLVING YOUR CHILD IN A VARIETY OF RECREATIONAL ACTIVITIES

Nursery-school-age children love to participate in games and activities such as cooking and baking. Perhaps you have heard a three- or four-year-old child tell an adult, "Watch me!" as he or she did a dance or prepared a make-believe meal. Now is the time to build rockets, barns, and garages out of the blocks and wooden logs in the toy chest.

You may want to get your child a sandbox and join your child as he or she makes sand castles or other shapes in the sand. If you enjoy roller-skating or ice-skating, take your child with you and share your enthusiasm for a sport. Your child may ask you to play "Ring Around the Rosy" and other games. If you don't know the game, ask your child to explain it to you. For additional help, books such as *Come With Us to Playgroup* (Magee & Ornstein), *Playthings* (Isenberg and Jacobs), and *What to Do When There's Nothing to Do* (Gregg) have many ideas for parents and adults.*

Since the three- or four-year-old enjoys imitating adults, you may want to let your child sort out toys, such as beads and blocks, or articles of clothing, such as socks. This will give your child further experience in recognizing matching colors and shapes (visual discrimination). Similarly, you may ask the child to join you in playing "sound detective." Both of you go about the house or yard searching for common sounds, such as running or dripping water, birds chirping, and so on. This will help the child to notice matching sounds (auditory

*Isenberg, Joan and Judith Jacob. *Playthings as Learning Tools.* New York: John Wiley & Sons, 1982. Magee, Patricia & Marilyn Ornstein. *Come With Us to Playgroup: A Handbook for Parents & Teachers of Young Children,* Englewood Cliffs, N.Y.: Prentice-Hall, Inc., 1981. Gregg, Elizabeth & Boston Children's Medical Center Staff. *What to Do When There's Nothing to Do.* New York: Dell Publishing Co., Inc., 1970.

discrimination). We've included an example of a "quiet fun book" that parents can make to use with their children. This book stresses visual discrimination.

Nursery-school-age children enjoy working with wooden puzzles. Ten to twelve pieces is the right size for a child of this age. Puzzles make fine birthday or holiday gifts. The two of you can play with the puzzle together, or he or she can manipulate the pieces alone. This activity will help your child to improve his or her visual skills and motor-control skills.

Three- to-four-year-olds enjoy dancing or moving to records, jingles, TV commercials, music boxes, radios, or repetitive nursery rhymes and phrases within a story. Songs such as "Hey, Betty Martin," "Itsy-Bitsy Spider," and "Skip to My Lou" have a simple melody and repeated phrases that allow the nursery-school-age child to skip, sway, or tiptoe while the adult and child sing the song. Many of Hap Palmer's records are useful with young children because they require them to bend their knees, bounce, hop, jump, or walk to music.

Most children this age enjoy art because it is a way to re-create the events or images in their lives. Their artwork reflects their own interpretations of their environment. Young children delight in tempera painting (using a water-soluble paint mixture) and watching what happens to the brush as they move it on the paper. The child may just make horizontal or vertical strokes with a variety of colors, or may actually attempt to make objects or people significant to them. As your child shares his or her artwork with you, don't expect to see perfect images of houses, trees, birds, or people. Instead, observe and appreciate the vibrant colors, varying brushstrokes, and imaginative shapes. Encourage your child to make more drawings or paintings, not fewer ones because they are not perfect or do not look as you expect them to. You can hang up your child's artwork and encourage your child to make something to send to grandparents or to a favorite aunt or uncle. As the child experiments with the pencil, crayon, or paintbrush in a playful or creative manner, he or she will mature in the ability to control his or her artwork.

Some children like to draw when they run out of other ways to play. One of the authors was working in her office one morning when two young children accompanied their mothers to the university. After playing with some building blocks, stuffed animals, and balls, the children decided to draw a picture for the author. Thea, aged three and a half, said, "This is a picture of a lady, and over here is a rocket. This is for you." April also talked about her picture: "This is a flower" (pointing to the center of the picture), "and there is a rainbow."

EDUCATIONAL PROGRAMS AVAILABLE FOR THREE- AND FOUR-YEAR-OLDS

By the time your child is three or four, you may want to have him or her spend part of the day in a nursery school. Nursery schools have educational programs especially planned to meet the needs of children three and four years of age. Nursery schools vary in the types of early-childhood programs provided. Some are run by church groups or civic clubs; others are sponsored by a group of parents and are known as "parent co-ops." Parent co-ops are organized, administered, and run by parents who volunteer their time on a regular basis to keep the school going. These schools offer half- or full-day programs for children twice a week, three days a week, or some other combination.

In each type of school, the young child has the opportunity

to learn and share experiences with other children of similar
age.

Typical half-day and full-day preschool schedules look like
this:

Half-Day Preschool Schedule

8:45 Arrival
9:00 Indoor or outdoor free-choice activities
9:50 Cleanup and bathroom routines
10:00 Snack
10:15 Indoor or outdoor free-choice activities
10:50 Cleanup
11:00 Music or movement activities
11:15 Story
11:30 Departure

Full-Day Preschool Schedule

7:00 Staggered arrival—indoor or outdoor free-choice
       activities
8:45 Cleanup and bathroom routines
9:05 Breakfast or light snack
9:30 Story and group meeting
9:40 Indoor or outdoor free-choice activities
10:40 Cleanup and bathroom routines
10:50 Indoor or outdoor free-choice activities
11:35 Cleanup
11:45 Music or movement activities
12:00 Cleanup and bathroom routines
12:10 Lunch
1:00 Routines
1:10 Coming together for group meeting/sharing/tell-a-
       story/naptime
3:00 Routines; put up cots
3:15 Snack
3:45 Indoor or outdoor free-choice activities
5:30 Staggered departure

(From Joan M. Bergstrom, Rose K. Margosian, and Frances A. Olson,
Enhancement of Growth and Learning for Young Children. Columbus, O.:
Charles E. Merrill Co., 1976, p. 91. Reprinted by permission.)

HOW CAN YOU SELECT A GOOD NURSERY SCHOOL?

Since there are a variety of educational programs to select from, you will want to do quite a bit of checking before making a final decision about the nursery school for your child. First of all, you need to decide why you want to place your child in an educational setting. Are you a working parent who needs to have your child cared for under supervision? Does your child need more of a challenge than he or she is receiving while at the day-care center or a private baby-sitter's home? Is your child shy and retiring? Does your child need the opportunity to be with others of his or her own age? Is the neighborhood one in which there are few children close to yours in age?

Not every child needs to be in a nursery school at age three or four. How can you tell whether you should send your child to nursery school?

One of the best ways to make a decision about whether your child is ready for nursery school is to observe him or her very carefully. Does your child ask questions and show an interest in learning more about the world outside your home? How does your child relate to other children his or her age? Does your child enjoy being with them and look forward to their visits? If so, you can begin to think about the right kind of nursery school for your child.

In selecting a nursery school, visit several to observe what goes on there. Talk with the director and some of the teachers. A decision should be based on real knowledge of the nursery school and how well the staff of that school will be able to accomplish what you want for your child. You may want to talk with some of your friends who have sent their children to a nursery school. You may also want to review information developed by several professional organizations that are concerned about helping parents select the very best care for their young children. Organizations such as the American Association of University Women, the Association for Childhood Education International, and the National Association for the Education of Young Children have developed a variety of aids to help parents make decisions about care for their preschool children.

One especially helpful publication developed by the National Association for the Education of Young Children lists specific questions to try to answer while observing at a nursery school. Among these questions are the following:

- Is there space for active play but still enough space where quiet play may go undisturbed, both indoors and out?
- Are safe, sanitary, and healthy conditions maintained?
- Is the child's health protected and promoted?
- Are there sufficient equipment and play materials readily available for the child's enjoyment and development?
- Are children helped to increase their use of language and to expand their concepts?
- Are opportunities provided for the child's social and emotional development?
- Are there enough adults to work with the group and to care for the needs of individual children?
- Do the adults enjoy and understand children?
- Does the center use all available community resources?

Using this set of questions when you visit a prospective nursery school should help you decide whether the nursery school is appropriate for your child.

HOW WILL A NURSERY SCHOOL CONTRIBUTE TO YOUR CHILD'S GROWTH AS A READER?

The major way in which a nursery school will help your child prepare to read is by providing a range of experiences in a setting in which your child will learn to relate to other children of the same age and to adults other than parents. A formal reading program is not appropriate for children three or four years of age. Let us explain why.

First of all, most children three or four years of age are not yet physically able to read. Their eyes have not matured to the point that they are able to adjust their focus from distance viewing to the close-up viewing needed for reading a page of print. They also are not yet ready to follow words from left to right, to make the required return sweep across the page at the end of a line of print, or to follow the printed symbols from top to bottom. In fact, some researchers believe that only 25 percent of our nation's kindergarten children are physiologically mature enough to enable them to accept formal reading instruction with ease. If this is true of kindergarteners, it is even more true of children three or four years of age.

A second reason why there should be no formal reading instruction in a nursery school for three- and four-year-old children is because a child of this age still has a great deal of social and emotional growing to do. A good nursery school provides children with time to be with other children, to learn to get along with them, and to test out ways of becoming a comfortable member of the group. Learning to become a contributing member of a group will give him or her the confidence needed to learn other tasks, such as reading, as the child moves into the primary grades.

Although we do not support formal reading programs for three- or four-year-old children, many important kinds of learning do take place in a good nursery school. For example, your child will have many opportunities to be involved in dramatic play alone as well as with other children. During this type of play, children use props that symbolize other things. Modeling dough might represent scrambled eggs; a rectangular block might represent a sandwich. Recent research has revealed that children who use these symbols in dramatic play are better able to handle the symbols involved in reading.

Most good nursery-school programs provide children with the opportunity to be involved in many self-directed activities which help develop skills that will be needed later in the formal reading program. For example, block-building contributes to improved eye-hand coordination.

In a good nursery school, there will be a great deal of reading done by the teacher, so that your child should gain a greater appreciation for the importance of reading. A major aspect of teaching a child to read is creating the desire to learn and helping a child learn that reading is a useful skill.

In most nursery schools, children are exposed to the importance of the written word in other ways as well. Signs, labels, and titles for their artwork will illustrate the uses of writing. As the child begins to show an interest in reading and writing, many nursery-school teachers may help the child to see the relationship between these two skills by writing down stories dictated by the child. Children are usually eager to read something they have written.

As you can see, in a good nursery school, a lot happens that will help prepare your child to read. However, the emphasis is on a balanced program appropriate for children three or four years of age rather than a narrow program that focuses on only one skill.

4

ACTIVITIES FOR THE KINDERGARTEN CHILD
AGES FOUR AND FIVE

In previous chapters, we have focused primarily on what you as a parent can do to provide your child with the kind of experiences that develop good readers. We've focused on you because until your child enters kindergarten, you are the most influential adult in your child's life.

When children enter school, another adult enters their lives: the kindergarten teacher. You are now sharing your responsibility for educating your child with a stranger in a setting that will be new to you and new to your child.

In this chapter, we will focus first on what will probably be happening to your child at school. Then we'll look at ways in which you can supplement and support these activities through your work with your child.

HOW CAN YOU FIND OUT ABOUT YOUR CHILD'S KINDERGARTEN?

Since 1873, when the first public-school kindergarten was established in St. Louis, Missouri, early-childhood educators have worked to establish programs for four- and five-year-olds that are based on our best knowledge of the young child. Today most states support public kindergartens. There is much diversity with regard to what takes place within each kindergarten classroom. That's why it is important for you to find out as much as possible about your child's kindergarten so that you will understand what is happening there and why these experiences are important.

Most schools or school systems prepare a handbook for parents of children entering school for the first time. A handbook of this kind might include basic information about goals, typical activities, and a schedule. The school's point of view about early reading experiences will also be presented. If possible, you should read such a handbook before visiting the school.

Many schools also conduct an orientation for parents at the school, often in your child's classroom. The orientation presents basic information that the school believes parents should have and gives parents the opportunity to raise questions. These meetings are usually scheduled at convenient times for parents who work outside the home. These are excellent times to get information, meet other parents, and ask questions. If you've attended an orientation, when your child brings items of schoolwork home or shares information about what is going on, you will understand it better.

WHAT IS A READING PROGRAM?

As we mentioned in Chapter 1, there are many ways to define reading. We define reading as an integral part of communication, which is a complex process that begins during infancy. Reading involves the recognition and interpretation of what is read in light of personal experiences. If readers do not get meaning from the printed words, they do nothing but pronounce words.

Prior to the mid-1960s, a mental age of 6.5 was thought to be necessary for success in beginning reading. Therefore, formal reading instruction was reserved for first-grade classrooms. However, recent research and experience with federally funded programs such as Head Start have shown that some children are now ready to begin formal reading instruction in kindergarten. Educators attribute the change to the influence of television, a wider background of preschool experiences, and the mobility of the modern family. These factors have helped some children to develop larger and more complex speaking vocabularies, which contribute to their readiness to read.

In Chapter 1, we discussed the three most prevalent points of view about reading readiness: (1) readiness as a specific stage of development, (2) readiness as a continuing process, and (3) readiness as a sequence of skills.

When you visit your child's school, you will want to learn more about the reading-readiness program provided in the kindergarten and the skills that are being developed through this program. To help you better understand these different viewpoints about reading readiness, we will describe the activities that you might find in classrooms where teachers have differing viewpoints about readiness.

Readiness as a specific stage of development. Kindergarten teachers who regard readiness as a specific stage of development generally view their year with the children as a readiness experience that prepares the children for formal reading instruction in the first grade. Such a teacher would provide a rich environment for your child, which would include play with trucks, blocks, dolls, dress-up clothes and housekeeping toys, physical activities on climbing and riding toys, and art, music, and stories.

Teachers with this viewpoint on readiness place a major emphasis on oral language and listening, as well as on using and extending the experiences that children bring to the kindergarten. Such teachers would also be most concerned with developing an interest in books and the pleasures of reading.

Readiness as a continuous process. Kindergarten teachers who view reading as a continuous process, which begins when children learn a language and ends with adult reading, believe that a child begins to learn a task with easy steps and progresses until he or she is quite proficient at the task. In such teachers' classrooms, you would see all of the activities described in the previous section, but these would be supplemented by an integrated language-arts program. This program would include conversation and language groups, listening activities, a writing center in which the children learn to name and write letters and numerals, and reading activities in which they learn sight words related to current interests and materials. This kind of teacher would be emphasizing the same readiness skills as the teacher who views readiness as a specific stage of development but would provide extra opportunities for those children who have revealed greater readiness for writing and reading instruction.

Readiness as a sequence of skills. Other kindergarten teachers view reading readiness as a sequence of skills or activities planned to prepare your child for a formal reading program. If your child's teacher interprets reading readiness from this point of view, he or she may explain to you the specific types of activities that have been planned to get your child ready for formal reading instruction in first grade. The materials used by such teachers would usually have been developed by the same authors who developed the first-grade reading program. Most children in the kindergarten class will work their way through these materials. Some children may even be moved into the first-grade reading program if the school system's philosophy permits it.

The skills emphasized in most formal reading-readiness programs are auditory discrimination, visual discrimination, and eye-hand coordination (or perceptual-motor skill). The other skills emphasized by the approaches previously mentioned are also included. In theory, once the children have mastered these skills, usually taught in a prescribed sequence, they are ready to move into a formal reading program.

WHICH READING-READINESS PROGRAM IS BEST?

We have no research evidence that supports one approach to reading readiness as more effective than the others. Children from all three types of programs have moved into formal reading programs in the primary grades and learned to read. We do prefer, however, to view reading readiness as a continuous process, and we believe in providing opportunities in kindergarten for children who are ready for structured writing and reading activities. Many other reading and childhood-education specialists support this viewpoint.

WHAT ABOUT THE EARLY READER?

Some children may actually be able to read and understand what they are reading before they enter kindergarten. When these children are asked how they learned to read, they are usually not able to explain their system, which most likely was developed by observation of older children in the family or through experiences provided by their parents. Usually children who learn to read early have above-average intelligence or have been raised in an environment where they were talked to a lot and had positive experiences with books. We must point out, however, that having above-average intelligence and being exposed to language and books is no guarantee that a child will read early.

If a child is able to pronounce written words and understand what he or she is reading before entering kindergarten, there are several ways in which the teacher might handle this unusual skill. These are the possibilities:

1. After using a standardized reading test to determine the child's level, the teacher might place him or her in a special class with first-graders for reading instruction. Although an adult might see this as something that would make the child feel very special, for some children this could be very unpleasant, since it involves separation from friends and classmates.
2. The teacher could group the advanced child with other children in the class who have similar skills.
3. The teacher could provide opportunities for the children to work independently, and, while the other children are busy, use this time to work with the advanced child on reading. The teacher would probably ask the child's parents to supplement the instruction with home activities, since time to work with the child individually would be limited.

If your child is an early reader, you will need to continue activities at home to help him or her enjoy reading, regardless of which option the teacher selects.

HOW CAN YOU WORK WITH YOUR KINDERGARTEN CHILD?

There are many activities you can do with your child that will relate directly to the readiness activities in your child's school. We have organized our discussion of these activities under the seven basic skills covered in many readiness programs: oral language; listening; experiential background; auditory discrimination; visual discrimination; perceptual-motor skills; and interest. The organization is designed to acquaint you with the terminology used by many kindergarten teachers when discussing their readiness programs. You will note, however, that these activities include the basic ingredients we emphasized in Chapters 2 and 3.

We've included more activities than you would probably want to do with your child. You can select those that seem best for you and your family. Be sensitive to your child's behavior when you are trying these activities. If your child seems bored, frustrated, or uninterested, he or she may be feeling pressured by having too much instruction, and it might be better to return to some of the activities discussed in earlier chapters of this book—reading aloud, talking about recent experiences, and so on.

ORAL-LANGUAGE ACTIVITIES

Purpose: These activities were selected to help your child learn to (1) repeat a sentence, (2) complete a sentence, and (3) express himself or herself in conversation.

Activity 1:

While talking to your child in a car, ask him or her to repeat a sentence after you. For example, you could make up sentences about things you see along the way. Keep the sentences short—four to six words. You could also do this while you are waiting in line at the grocery store or a department store. (A modification of this activity is to have the children make up sentences on their own.)

Activity 2:

Here's something fun to do with mateless socks. Put an object into a sock and tie the top. Number the sock with a magic marker. Do this with up to ten socks and objects. Put them all in a cardboard box. Ask your child to feel the object inside the sock, name the object, and tell you what it could be used for. For example, when feeling a wooden block, your child would say: "This is a block. A block is to build things with." It would be wise to list on the box the object in each numbered sock so you will know what is in each sock.

Activity 3:

Cut pictures out of magazines and catalogs; to make them more permanent, paste them on cardboard or note cards. Place these pictures in a paper bag. Let your child reach into the bag and pull out a picture. Have your child tell you a sentence about the picture after looking at it for a few minutes. Your child can tell you about the actions visible in the picture or anything else he or she wants to say about the picture. If your child wants to, let him or her tell you a story about it.

Activity 4:

Read a story to your child and discuss it. Ask the child to tell you how he or she would change it if the child were the author. The child could change the ending, change a character, or even change the setting.

Activity 5:

Have your child dictate a letter to a relative who lives out of town. If you want, you can record the message on a tape cassette.

Activity 6:

Recite short nursery rhymes or riddles and have your child repeat them. The ones you will most likely remember will be those from your own childhood. This is a good opportunity to share some of your childhood memories with your child.

Activity 7:

Involve your child in housekeeping routines by giving the child directions to do something. Then have him or her talk about what is being done. For example, say to the child: "Johnny, put this magazine on the coffee table." As Johnny does this, he would say: "I'm putting this magazine on the coffee table."

You can probably think of many more ways to accomplish the goals listed at the beginning of this section, as well as variations on these seven activities.

LISTENING ACTIVITIES

Purpose: These activities were selected to help your child learn to (1) follow simple directions, (2) recall a simple sequence of events, and (3) recall a story he or she has heard.

Activity 1:

Tell your child a favorite folk or fairy tale. You probably have at least one that is a special favorite of yours. Ask your child to retell the story in his or her words. After learning the story, your child can have a lot of fun telling it to other people and asking them to share one of their favorites. This could be the beginning of a family custom of sharing favorite stories that everyone would enjoy.

Activity 2:

While you are in the kitchen preparing a meal, if your child is bored or disturbing you, play a game of identifying kitchen sounds. Have him or her turn away with closed eyes and name the different sounds heard, such as running water, the opening and closing of the refrigerator, and so on.

Activity 3:

To help your child learn to listen to and follow simple directions, take advantage of such situations as mealtimes and bedtimes, when regular routines need to be reinforced with reminders. For example, you might say: "Put your dishes in the sink and put your chair under the table," or "Take off your school clothes and put on your nightclothes."

Activity 4:

Take a walk around your neighborhood. Ask your child to listen to some of the sounds he or she may hear. When you are back home, talk about your trip. For example, you may have heard a power saw. Talk about what a power saw is and what it does. You may have heard chattering squirrels. You might talk about the fact that the squirrels are preparing for winter and that they chatter with each other as they gather nuts.

EXPERIENTIAL BACKGROUND

Purpose: These activities are selected to encourage your child to (1) develop background experiences which will be resources for reading and (2) tell about daily routines or special activities with his or her spoken vocabulary.

Activity 1:

Look for books at a grocery store, drugstore, garage sale, or library that picture working people with whom your child has had some contact, such as the mail carrier, baker, police officer, firefighter, sanitation worker, and so on. Have your child compare the pictures in the book with real people seen in the neighborhood.

Activity 2:

When you're at the park, help your child expand his or her vocabulary by referring to the objects by name: swing, hobby horse, teeter-totter, slide, and so on. You can also talk about other sights in the park: the fence that encloses it, the trees that grow there, the grass, and so on. A trip on the bus or the subway could also encourage a discussion about words.

Activity 3:

As you prepare a meal, talk about the fruits, vegetables, and meats you are using. Talk about where they come from and how they grow.

Activity 4:

When you're waiting someplace with your child, talk about other places he might like to be. For example, if you're waiting in a doctor's office, he or she might prefer to be at the zoo. Your child could tell you what he or she might see there and what would be best about the trip.

Activity 5:

After your child has finished playing, ask him or her to put away the playthings. You can use this as a learning experience by asking your child to put away the items you identify. For example, ask your child to put away the "smallest thing," the "largest thing," the "softest thing," the "thinnest thing," and so on.

Activity 6:

Because young children often confuse real experiences with imaginary ones from their own fantasies or from television, talk about both in order to help your child begin to understand the differences between the two. For example, on a program like *Mister Rogers' Neighborhood,* the children take a trip to "the neighborhood of make-believe," where they do and see things that could not happen in real life. The rest of the program, however, is realistic and depicts common experiences that many boys and girls have. Helping children to be able to talk about and distinguish between real and imaginary experiences is important and valuable.

AUDITORY DISCRIMINATION

Purpose: These activities were selected to enable your child to (1) hear likenesses and differences in words, (2) recognize rhyming words and words that begin with the same sounds, and (3) repeat one-syllable, two-syllable, and three-syllable words.

Activity 1:

Have your child sit facing away from you so that he or she cannot see your lips while you are speaking. Pronounce three or four pairs of words and ask your child to tell you whether the words are alike or different. For example: *bat-bat; dog-dog; man-nest; funny-penny.* As your child begins to understand this activity, you can increase the number of word pairs to about ten. If you have a tape recorder, the words could be recorded on tape. Be sure to pause after each word pair so that your child has time to respond.

Activity 2:

While talking to your child, ask him or her to listen to three words. Explain that one of the three words is different. Ask your child to tell you which word is different. For example: *cat-bat-cat; bug-bug-bed; pan-pop-pop.* This is a good activity to do while riding in a car. Highway signs and advertisements can help you think of words to use in this three-word listening activity.

Activity 3:

Select several pictures from the newspaper or a magazine. Place them on the kitchen table or floor. While you and your child are looking at the pictures, say something about one of them and then ask your child to point to the one about which you are talking. Continue to do this until you have talked about all of the pictures. To be sure that your child is listening carefully, you might make a statement about a picture you used before.

Activity 4:

When your child is trying to find something to do, ask him or her to look around the room for things that begin with a letter that has been introduced at school. For example, if you are in the bedroom, you might ask him or her to look for things that begin with *b.* Your child might find a bed, a button, a buckle, and so on.

Activity 5:

Ask your child to become a "word detective" by listening for new words on television and radio, especially during the commercials. Ask your child to tell you some of the new words in a listening game. Either say the same word twice or use it with another word to form a word pair.

Activity 6:

Find a poem that you like that has rhyming words. After reading it to your child, talk about how the poet selected certain words to make the poem sound nice. Give an example of two words that rhyme. Read the poem again and ask the child to identify other words that rhyme.

VISUAL DISCRIMINATION

Purpose: These activities have been selected to help your child to (1) recognize likenesses and differences in words, (2) recognize letters, and (3) recognize words.

Activity 1:

Cut out fifty-two two-inch squares of paper. Divide them into two stacks of twenty-six. Put a letter of the alphabet on each square, written as capital letters (A, B, C, and so on). Separate the two sets and place them in envelopes or two small paper bags. From each envelope or bag, remove the same five letters of the alphabet. Place them on top of the table in separate stacks. Then take one letter from your stack and ask the child to find one in his stack that matches yours. Keep doing this until all five have been used. Now choose five more. After the child learns to recognize more and more letters, he can play this game with the total set of alphabet squares.

Activity 2:

Find a page of advertisements in the newspaper or in your mail. Using a crayon or magic marker, circle a letter on the advertisement. Then have your child use a different color crayon to circle as many other examples of the same letter on the page as possible. When your child has finished, check his or her work and circle another letter.

Activity 3:

Construct a temporary letter mobile for each letter of the alphabet your child has learned at school. Cut out a shape from a piece of cardboard or construction paper. Print the letter on the shape. Now ask the child to find or draw two or three pictures of objects that begin with that letter. Punch a hole in the shape and in the pictures your child provides. Using yarn or string, attach the pictures to the shape and hang the mobile from the ceiling, on a doorknob, or in any convenient place where your child can enjoy it.

Activity 4:

Using six envelopes and a package of multicolored construction paper, you can construct a game to help your child distinguish colors. Cut two 2 × 2-inch squares from six different colors of construction paper. Paste one square of each color on the outside of each envelope. Then ask your child to put each of the remaining squares into the envelope with the matching color.

Activity 5:

Take the back of a tablet or a 5 × 8-inch index card and draw lines on it to make three rows with four spaces on each. Then draw capital letters on each line. Make sure that you have two letters on each line that match. Ask your child to draw a line between the two letters that are the same.

Activity 6:

Draw lines on a sheet of plain paper so that you have four rows of three boxes. Put the same shape (don't use circles and squares) in each row, but put one of those shapes facing a different direction. Ask your child to point to or place a marker on the shape in each row that is not the same as the others.

PERCEPTUAL-MOTOR SKILLS

Purpose: These activities were selected to help your child to (1) recognize left and right, (2) recognize his or her name in print, (3) recognize left to right eye movement, (4) recognize top to bottom, and (5) recognize the front and back of a book.

Activity 1:

Print the letters of the alphabet on 3 × 5-inch cards or on cardboard squares. Using these letters, make words for the child to read to you. As you make a word, say each letter individually to indicate the sequence of letters. Use simple words such as *MOM, DAD,* your child's name, *SUN, MILK, CAT,* and *DOG.* Place them one under the other in a list to get across the idea that they are single words and not a sentence.

Repeat each word and have your child repeat it after you. You can also use magnetic letters placed on the refrigerator at the height of the child.

Activity 2:

Find an easy-to-read book and move your child's finger along the print as you read it to him or her. After you have finished a page, ask if your child recognized any of the words on the page. Ask him or her to point to them and repeat them for you.

Activity 3:

After a special holiday or a birthday, encourage your child to "write" thank-you notes for gifts received from friends and relatives. Your child can tell you what he or she wants to say in the note, while you do the actual printing. Let your child sign the note at the bottom. Keep the note simple and just one or two sentences long.

Activity 4:

Find a comic strip in the newspaper that has three or four pictures, preferably one without words, such as "Ferdinand" or "Henry." Paste the strip on a piece of cardboard and number each picture on the reverse side. Then cut up the comic strip and mix up the pictures. Ask your child to put the pictures in the correct sequence from left to right. After you have finished with the game, place it in an envelope so that your child can use it again. Your child also might like to help you make other games like this one.

Activity 5:

Find a page in a magazine or a catalog with several pictures on it. Ask your child to point to the object that you name. Ask him to tell you where it is on the page; for example, "The ball is at the top of the page," "The doll is at the bottom of the page," or "The truck is on the right side of the page."

Activity 6:

Read with your child a book about the seasons. Talk with your child about the months that make up the seasons. On the family calendar, show your child how a month is made up of weeks and a week is made up of days. Move your finger from Sunday through Saturday of one week, and have your child do the same. From time to time, talk about the calendar and ask your child to help you count the days left in a week, a month, or a season. You could also make or purchase a calendar for the child's personal use.

INTEREST

Purpose: These activities have been selected to maintain the child's interest in letters, words, and other reading activities.

Activity 1:

While visiting the library, ask your child to try to find some of the picture books that he or she has seen or heard read in kindergarten class. Take a few books home. When you get home, read one book to your child and talk about the things in the book that he or she likes best: the plot, the characters, the pictures, the sounds of the words.

Activity 2:

Because reading and writing are so closely connected, your child may begin to ask you to spell words so that he or she can make up original stories. Encourage your child if such an interest develops. Some children "write" their own stories without anyone's help, and although the spelling may be unusual, they know what they are saying. Don't worry about correcting the spelling or the grammar. The ideas are more important at this stage. If your child asks you how to spell a word for a story, write it on a piece of paper and then repeat each letter to be sure your writing can be copied correctly. When your child has finished the story, encourage him or her to illustrate it. Then display it in a place where your child can read it again alone or to others.

Activity 3:

After seeing a program on television about a particular topic or storybook character, your child may ask you to take him or her to find a book about the topic or character. After you have read the book, ask your child to retell the story. Your child could take the book to school to share with the other kindergarten children. Perhaps the teacher can read it to the class.

Activity 4:

Find some recipes that are easy to read and to follow. You could write them yourself, or use a book such as *What to Do with . . . a Fruit* by Françoise Blanchet and Rinke Dornekamp (Woodbury, New York: Barron's Educational Series, 1979). Read the directions for the recipe to your child and help him or her follow it step by step. This is a practical reading experience with a very pleasant ending.

MORE ACTIVITIES

As we have mentioned in earlier chapters, there are many things you do in your home that can be used as learning experiences for your child. These incidental opportunities for learning are part of your daily lives—grocery shopping, cleaning house, taking children to and from meetings in a car—and can be used to build on the experiences that your child will be having in school. You may also be eager to go beyond the ordinary daily experiences and help your children to learn through books, games, toys, and visits to special places.

In both situations, parents can use their time with their child in a way that will be beneficial to the child's reading readiness.

An example of an incidental opportunity would be when you are shopping in a grocery store. Kindergarten children often love to shop with their parents, and even though they can sometimes become a nuisance because of their eagerness to explore and to select items they want, this is a great opportunity for them to grow in skills that their teacher has introduced at school, such as selecting, identifying, categorizing, and classifying objects. This is how a mother might use part of her shopping time:

MOTHER: Can you find something down the aisle that is round?

JOHNNY: (running down the aisle) Look, Mom! I found some candy that is round.

MOTHER: Good. Let's go to the next aisle and see what we can find on my shopping list that is round. Put the candy back on the shelf, Johnny.

This can be done with colors, vegetables, sizes of print, or favorite brands of products. (In fact, many people who are new to our country or have not learned to read identify products by shape, size, and color and seem to get along quite well.)

An example of a parent going beyond the ordinary, daily experiences might be using a lotto game with one's children. Lotto is played with a set of cards with separate pairs of matching pictures. This game may not seem very exciting to you, but by playing the game, a child can demonstrate that he or she is becoming independent and can do things that take intelligence and thought. This game can provide hours of enjoyment for a child with parents or alone.

This is how a father might use a lotto game with his child:

FATHER: Susie, can you name some of the pairs of pictures that you have just matched?

SUSIE: Yes! There are oranges, lettuce, apples, peas, pears, carrots, bananas, celery, potatoes, and beans.

FATHER: Correct! Now I'll ask you another question. Can you tell me the names of all the vegetables?

SUSIE: They are lettuce, peas, carrots, celery, potatoes, and beans.

FATHER: Very good, Susie. You really know lots of vegetables. I bet that you've seen these at the grocery store when you go shopping with us.

As you can see, this father is doing nothing more than talking with his child about the game and using their discussion to refer to previous experiences that his daughter has had with some of the items in the lotto game. He could draw upon many other of her experiences: books she has seen at nursery school or the library, trips to her grandparents, and TV programs she has seen, for example.

If Susie was not able to identify some of the objects by name, her father could do several things. For instance, he could use a picture dictionary, if one is available in the home, and look through it with the child for the names of the objects the child could not identify. Susie could hold the unidentified card while she and her father looked in the book to find the right name of the object. When Susie found the picture, her father could read the description, use the word in a sentence, and then ask Susie to use the word in a sentence. The major emphasis should be on having Susie repeat the word until she becomes familiar with its sound and associates it with the picture. Although this takes time, the child learns that one can use books to find information about things. At first children may need a parent's help, but later they may use the books alone.

DO ALL CHILDREN BENEFIT FROM KINDERGARTEN READING-READINESS PROGRAMS?

As we mentioned earlier, your child has been getting ready to read since infancy. You have contributed to that process because of your purposeful interaction with him or her. By the end of kindergarten, however, your child may still not be ready to read, in spite of everything you and the teacher have done. Even if you are disappointed, try not to pass these feelings on to your child. Many children are not ready to read—even if they have been through a formal reading-readiness program—until second grade or later.

5

ACTIVITIES FOR THE
FIRST-GRADE CHILD
AGES FIVE AND SIX

Can you remember what you were like when you were in the first grade? You probably have a few pictures around that your parents took. But do you remember what you *felt* like when you left kindergarten or nursery school to enter "real" school?

Children bring a lot of anxiety with them to school. What will the teacher be like? Will they find a friend? Will they be expected to read immediately, or will they actually be taught this mysterious skill? What will their parents think of them if they don't learn to read? Why do some of their friends already know how to read? Is there something wrong with them?

Although your first-grader may look cool and collected when you prepare him or her for the first day of school, if you can remember any of your own feelings about going to first grade, you have some idea of how they are feeling.

WHAT ARE FIRST-GRADERS LIKE?

Six-year-old children are curious and enthusiastic. They want to learn more and more about this interesting world around them and now, more than ever before, they see books as a source of knowledge as well as entertainment. During these years the school and public libraries become much more important to them as a way of helping them to make sense of their sometimes puzzling world.

First-grade children are, of course, all different, but the following characteristics will give you a general idea of what they may be expected to do. First-graders

- have a natural inclination for physical activity; boys especially find it hard to sit still for any length of time.

- are moving toward greater independence and at times seem to be at war with everyone, especially parents.
- have difficulty making up their minds.
- are often involved in fights.
- have frequent tantrums.
- can also be fearful, shy, and insecure.
- are very interested in sex.
- may take advantage of learning to read by entertaining themselves with books.
- enjoy records, and games such as Chinese checkers.
- have a stronger sense of right and wrong than ever before, although they may find it difficult to do what they agree is right.
- have a hard time meeting the expectations of the adults in their lives.
- are moving through many physical and emotional changes.
- are skilled at giving and receiving information.
- communicate well with family, friends, and strangers.
- take part appropriately in a conversation.
- speak in sentences whose grammar is little different from that of an adult.
- need to learn such grammatical fine points as subject-verb agreement and some irregular past-tense verbs.

FIRST-GRADE READING INSTRUCTION

Even if a child has been in kindergarten or nursery school, there is still something very special about first grade. Children know that it is during first grade that most of them will learn to read.

According to current research, most children are ready to begin formal instruction in reading in the first grade. Some educators and psychologists believe that a formal reading program should be delayed until second or third grade. But your child will most likely begin formal reading instruction in the early months of first grade.

You'll recall that earlier in this book you read there is no one method of teaching reading that works for every child. The various methods or approaches of teaching reading could be compared to the numerous recipes for baking brownies or chocolate-chip cookies. The cookie recipes use different ingredients, yet generally speaking, the cookies are tasty. Similarly, most children learn to read regardless of the method used.

Several years ago, the United States Office of Education did a study of first-grade teachers to learn whether there was one best approach to the teaching of reading. The researchers concluded that the key to a successful reading program was not the method but the attitude and skill of the teacher using the method.

Do you remember the approach that was used to teach you to read? If you learned to read during the years 1940–60, you may have learned to read from a textbook with realistic and vividly illustrated stories like the one shown on the next page. (The reproductions of illustrations from children's books are intended to show the general text and design only. We obviously could not reproduce them in full color.) Does it bring back memories? These textbooks, known as basal readers, combined the teaching of reading and literature. There were relatively few words introduced in these readers, but the words were used in many different contexts so that they had more meaning for the student. You may have used supplementary materials in the form of workbooks designed for individual and group work.

The years since 1960 have seen many changes in the

teaching of reading. The age at which reading is introduced, the instructional materials, and the methods of teaching and evaluation have all changed, but the most commonly used material for teaching is still the basal reader. When you go to your child's school for an orientation, the approach to reading that will be used will probably be explained. Three of the most popular current approaches are described below. These approaches are (1) the basal approach, (2) the language experience approach, and (3) the individualized approach.

THE BASAL READING APPROACH

In the United States the basal reading approach is the most popular method. Generally speaking, in this method the "mechanics" of reading are taught through a sequential development of skills. A set of books called basal readers are used. They increase in difficulty from a readiness or prereading level through sixth or eighth grade. Along with the readers children typically use a workbook specially designed to reinforce the skills taught in each basal reader.

While the basal reader is used as the primary source of reading in most classrooms, basal readers differ in their basic

Come to Play

"Run, Peggy," said Don.
"Run, run, little Buster.
Come here to play."

"Oh, Buster," said Peggy.
"We go to play."

"Look, Tad," said Don.
"Run here to play."

"See Kitty," said Peggy.
"Kitty comes to play.
Here comes little Bunny.
Bunny comes to play."

philosophy. There are three common reading philosophies followed by most basal readers: (1) the look-say (the whole or analytic approach), (2) the phonics (also called synthetic or "sound out" approach), and (3) the linguistic approach.

When you visit your child's classroom you may find a familiar scene—children using workbooks and basal readers during their reading instruction. This scene may bring back memories from your schooldays or those of your younger sister, brother, or cousin. In fact, this type of basal reader has been used since the McGuffey readers of the 1840s.

The book companies that publish basal readers employ teams of experts to produce the books. In addition to using recent research, the company spends much money and time in producing the series.

As you browse through your child's basal reader, you will notice some changes in it from the one you remember using. These are just a few of the changes that have been made in basal readers since the 1960s.

1. The story content is richer. No longer is the white, middle-class family the dominant cast of characters. Now the stories are multicultural and multiethnic in nature. Various types of literature are used. For example, poetry, fables, biographies, and other kinds of nonfiction are used in addition to fiction.
2. The artwork is more dynamic. In addition to the realistic pictures, one now sees maps, charts, diagrams, photographs, cartoons, and abstract art.
3. The vocabulary is richer than it used to be. Although vocabulary control still exists, many more words are introduced throughout the series.
4. The format has become more flexible. Traditionally, the basal series started with one or more readiness books, one or more preprimers, a primer, and a first reader. For second and third grade there were two books per level, and one book each year for the fourth, fifth, and sixth grades. Each book was marked with the grade level in which the book would typically be used. The basal reader series ended with the sixth-grade level. Today the books are labeled in a variety of ways. Some are marked as levels one through

fourteen or fifteen, while others are marked as levels one through twenty-four. The idea is to avoid the notion that a book is only useful for one grade level.

5. Additional materials have been added. Besides the book and workbook, students now use: duplicating master worksheets that provide additional practice of the skills present at each level; mastery tests, to indicate the children's achievement of the skills taught at each level; and supplementary materials, which vary with each publishing company. Some feature games, others literature kits or minibooks that can be used to help children as they progress through the basal reader in the series.

The following publishers produce reading programs like these:

Allyn & Bacon
American Book Company
Ginn & Company
Harcourt Brace Jovanovich
Harper & Row
Holt, Rinehart & Winston
Houghton Mifflin
Laidlaw
Macmillan
Rand McNally
Scott, Foresman

The Look-Say Approach

The "look-say" approach is a method in which words are introduced to students in conversation, printed on the blackboard or on strips of paper, and then pronounced without intensive stress on phonics. The students begin to understand the association between letters and sounds, and spoken and printed words by looking at the words and then pronouncing them. Two examples are shown on the following pages.

Lucy was a busy worker.
She painted a lot of nice pictures.
She was a good reader.
And she liked to put things away.

But Lucy had one problem.
She did not listen.

Once the students learn to recognize words they learn to read phrases and sentences and short stories in paperback books. Then they progress to a hardback book.

A typical look-say (analytic) basal reader lesson takes several days to complete. The following sequence is usually followed:

1. *Introduction of vocabulary.* The core vocabulary of each story is introduced, and words previously learned are reinforced. The teacher also establishes a background for reading the story.
2. *Silent reading.* The teacher guides reading of the story after discussing the story setting. Prereading questions are used, such as, "What will the goat do next?" Read the next page to find out. Children read the section silently until the entire story is read.

3. *Oral reading.* The children read aloud to answer the prereading questions.
4. *Skill building.* Students complete exercises in the workbook. The skills introduced in the story are reinforced by these exercises.
5. *Supplemental activities.* The teacher extends the experiences by means of enrichment activities, such as drawing, reading other stories that relate to the same topic, and listening to records.

Some of the strengths of the look-say approach are:

1. There is a systematic plan for the development of word recognition, comprehension, and vocabulary skills.
2. The program is developed by experts. The teacher follows a teacher's guide, which provides activities and a step-by-step outline for teaching.
3. It's a well-developed program that progresses step by step in easy stages from prereading levels to sixth or eighth grade.
4. Vocabulary is presented and extended through the series. Workbooks and stories provide practice of this basic vocabulary.

Some of the weaknesses of the look-say approach are:

1. It is expensive. To purchase all the materials that accompany the program produced by a publishing company is very expensive.

2. It is too structured. Teachers trying to follow the teacher's guide may find it difficult to provide individualized instruction.
3. It is unrealistic. Stories do not show the stresses and strains of daily life.

You may expect to see some worksheets that your child has been given during class. From time to time you may be asked to go over these worksheets with your child or to verify that he or she has completed the worksheets at home. You may also receive word lists and be asked to review with your child the words contained in the list. School systems vary in their policy about what parents may be asked to do to reinforce the skills taught at school.

The Phonics Approach

If your child is in a phonics approach basal program, he or she will use basal readers and workbooks during first grade. In the phonics approach program, children are taught to read by first learning the letters representing certain sounds and then blending the sounds together to make words. The children combine this knowledge with writing and spelling, and they read stories that come from literature.

The materials used will vary with the company that produces them. For instance, if your child uses the Lippincott Basic Reading program, your child will progress through four books—a preprimer, a primer, and a first and second reader, plus a workbook for each reader. An excerpt from the Lippincott program appears on the next page.

If your child is using the Open Court reading program, he or she will first go through a foundation program made up of several softbound workbooks and then continue into a hardbound reader with an accompanying workbook. These materials provide your child with exercises that reinforce the language-arts skills.

In both of these programs there are additional materials, such as duplicating masters, magazines, kits, and flash cards which your child may be using.

The key point to remember about the phonics approach is that children are first taught the relationship between sounds and letters. Children learn to memorize the sounds of the language by jingles, songs, or clue pictures.

Therefore, if you were to visit your child's class in the initial phase of this approach, you would hear the teacher introducing the sounds and their spellings in isolation and then blending them into words. For example, you might hear the child say "but, oh, tuh" as he or she "sounds out" the word "boat."

As the child progresses through the school year, the teacher would probably follow a basic plan which would include the following:

1. *Introduction.* The teacher presents the background of the story to be read.
2. *Procedure.* The words found in the "Words to Watch" box are presented to the children.
3. *Expanding word concepts.* The teacher presents the words under the following categories: people, descriptive words, things, verbs, and miscellaneous. (Diacritical marks are used when presenting the words to the class.)
4. *Guided reading for comprehension.* The teacher presents the story and motivates the children to read it.

m M

man   mad   mud   am   drum

Nan and Dan run to the man.
R-r-rum, dum, dum!
R-r-rum, dum, dum!

5. *Extended reading skills*. The students read the story silently. Then they do the guided oral reading portion of the lesson and discuss it.
6. *Language arts*.
7. *Enrichment*.
8. *Suggestions for further activities*.

These last three components vary with the teacher and his or her class.

Some of the strengths of the phonics approach are:

1. Children have the language background and experiences to decode almost any words they may encounter in reading.
2. Children can read varied types of literature at earlier levels because there is little vocabulary control within the stories.
3. In the initial phase of instruction, students learn one sound and all of its spellings in one lesson.

Some of the weaknesses of the phonics approach are:

1. The heavy initial emphasis on the association between letters and the sounds they represent may influence children to rely on phonics as the sole means of decoding an unfamiliar word in a sentence.
2. Some phonics-trained children with good word-recognition skills may have poor comprehension skills because they have the idea that reading is merely sounding out words. The initial emphasis on pronunciation does not stress comprehension.
3. Some children may have trouble understanding what they are reading. The sentences are sometimes long and complicated due to the various types of literature used.
4. Not all the children using these materials can progress at the pace required to cover all the lessons and books in first grade.
5. Some phonics-trained children lack a large sight vocabulary (words that can be recognized on sight) because they rely on analyzing the sounds of the words when reading.

You may expect to see some worksheets that your child may need either to review or complete. Your child's teacher may suggest more specific things for you to do at home. At the scheduled teacher conferences at the school, you will learn more about the reading program, your child's progress, and what you can do to help make learning to read enjoyable for your child.

The Linguistics Approach

If your child is in a linguistics approach basal program, he or she will be using basal texts, workbooks, and supplementary materials. These materials are designed in line with the general belief that reading instruction centers on language, specifically the sound patterns of English.

The pioneer of this method was Leonard Bloomfield, a linguist, who recommended that reading instruction should start with teaching the identification of all alphabet letters by name, not by sound. Words in which each letter represents only one phonemic value are taught first; words with silent letters or less common sounds are avoided, so that the beginning words consist of three letters in a consonant-vowel-consonant pattern containing only short vowels. Bloomfield further urged use of the principle of "minimal variation," involving a list of words alike except for one letter, such as *ban, Dan, can, fan, man,* and the like. Rules about letter-sound correspondences should not be taught, according to Bloomfield, as the children will evolve correct responses when sounds and spelling correspond in regular fashion. Finally, the students employ learned words in sentences, such as *Nan can fan Dan.*

In the linguistics program, then, children are first taught to name the letters in alphabetical order. They then learn lists of words that follow regular spelling rules and learn to read sentences and stories that use these regularly spelled words. These stories may not be very interesting, because the vocabulary used in them is so highly controlled. Next the students learn the semiregular and irregular words. Once these are mastered, the students will read stories that are more interesting, and the teacher will now stress getting meaning from print. In other words, comprehension skills are taught after the students master the sound patterns used in language. A sample story appears on the following page.

Pat and Mom

Can Pat plan a swim trip?
If Pat helps Mom, Pat can.
Pat acts in a rush.
Swish! Pat gets the dishrag.
Splash! Pat plumps the pots
  in the dishpan.
Rub and scrub, Pat.
Pat's swift, but a dish
  slips from Pat's hand. Crash!
Brush it up, Pat;
  dump it in the trash.
Mom steps in. Mom helps Pat
  and Pat gets a swim.

Bloomfield's approach has been modified over the years. Today the most commonly used linguistics-oriented materials published are the *Merrill Linguistic Readers* (Charles E. Merrill Publishing Company) and the *Miami Linguistic Readers* (D. C. Heath & Company).

Some advantages of the linguistics approach are:

1. Children are taught the relationships between the sound and letter patterns that appear in normal English.
2. The words introduced in the early levels illustrate predictable, controlled sound-spelling patterns, and the irregular spellings are presented last.
3. Children do no sounding and blending exercises, because emphasis is placed on whole words. Children are expected to discover for themselves the relationship between sounds and letters.
4. This approach capitalizes on children's knowledge of oral language.

Some of the weaknesses of the linguistics approach are:

1. The lack of emphasis on comprehension in the early stages of the program.

2. The stress on learning the names of the letters in the alphabet in the initial stages of instruction.
3. The vocabulary in the stories in the lower levels in contrived, since it is controlled by the sound-spelling patterns being taught in a particular lesson. The vocabulary does not reflect the rich and diverse spoken vocabulary of children.
4. Due to learning problems, some children cannot discover the relationship of words to letters on their own. In other words, if they see *bat, fat,* and *cat,* they cannot see that the only difference among these words is a single initial letter.

If your child is learning to read in a linguistic basal reading program, the classroom teacher may ask your cooperation in reviewing some of your child's word lists and worksheets.

THE LANGUAGE EXPERIENCE APPROACH
Teachers who use the language experience approach believe that reading, as one aspect of the child's total language development, should be taught in conjunction with listening, speaking, and writing. In this approach, the child's oral language and life experiences form the basic structure around which the reading program is built. It's a process of getting meaning from print. The basic premise of the approach can be expressed in the words: "What I think about I can talk about. What I can talk about I can express in painting and writing. What I write I can read."

In a classroom where the language experience approach is being used, you would find paintings and drawings done by the children along with stories they had written as a group or as individuals. These are referred to as "experience charts." They record an experience of either the group or an individual child.

A visitor to the classroom might be an experience that could be written about by the class. After the visitor has left, the teacher would guide the children in a discussion of what happened. The children would dictate what they would like to write. The teacher would then read the dictated sentences back to the children so that they could make changes. The story would then be recopied on a chart or in some other permanent form and kept for future use. Here is a story written by four children.

A Boy, A Dog and A Frog

One day there was a boy who went to look for a frog. He saw a frog and the frog saw him. He was on the lily pad. The boy tripped over the log and fell into the water. The dog went in head first too. The boy was mad.

Then the frog jumped off a log and the boy went into the water again. The boy tried to catch the frog with a net but he caught the dog instead. He got mad and went home. The frog was sad because he didn't have anyone to have fun with. The frog followed their tracks. He saw the boy and the dog in the tub. The frog jumped into the tub on the dog's head. The frog was happy because he was with friends.

The End!

This approach also allows a child to record a personal experience in a drawing or a painting and then to talk about the picture with the teacher. The child would dictate a statement or two about the picture for the teacher to record. A sample of an individual story follows:

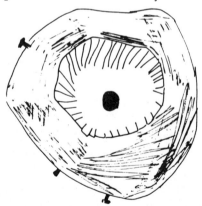

This is a fire alarm.
It is loud.
It is gray.
It means fire.

After the children have painted, talked, and dictated experiences to the teacher, several children may get together to read their stories to each other. As the year progresses, the children begin to write their own stories without the aid of the teacher and share them in small groups.

From their own experience stories, the children then move to some of the books in the classroom library and soon realize that they can read these writings just as they could the stories that they wrote themselves.

Although it may seem that the language experience approach would be appropriate only for beginning readers, those who have developed this approach use it for readers at all levels because of its many advantages. These include the following:

1. The language experience approach is highly personalized and individualized.
2. It uses the child's oral language as the basic source for word recognition and vocabulary.
3. Vocabulary can be introduced faster because it is not controlled, as in a basal reader.
4. It fosters creativity and independence.
5. It stresses communication, meaning, and comprehension.

Some of the disadvantages attributed to the language experience approach are as follows:

1. The teaching of word attack skills may be slighted. Word attack skills are strategies that a reader uses to recognize or "unlock" an unfamiliar word. For example:
   • Sight clues—the shape of a word or picture clues found on the page.
   • Phonics—"sounding out" a word.
   • Context clues—reading the rest of the sentence to see if you can guess the unfamiliar word that would make sense in the sentence or in the story.
   • Structural analysis—studying the parts of a word; "boys" has the root word "boy" in it.
2. Children who act as if they are reading may not be making the necessary "sound-symbol" relationships.
3. The lack of a clear sequential approach may cause confusion.

THE INDIVIDUALIZED READING APPROACH

By the time children enter first grade, they differ by several years in their reading levels. Some were able to read before entering kindergarten, others learned to read in kindergarten, while still others have just reached the point where they are ready to begin reading instruction. The individualized approach to reading was developed as a way of recognizing these differences in children's development by planning with and for each child individually.

The characteristics usually associated with the individualized reading program are the following:

1. Self-selection of books.
2. Individual pupil-teacher conferences.
3. Self-pacing in reading.
4. Record-keeping.
5. Availability of a wide variety of books and other reading materials.

Teachers using this approach would do a very careful analysis of the interests and abilities of the children in their classes. They would confer with the school librarian to select the right books for the children. This is usually done in an individual conference with each pupil, during which the teacher checks on word recognition, vocabulary development, comprehension, and other skills involved in learning to read. Records of the strengths and weaknesses of each pupil are kept.

Teachers who use this approach must be particularly competent in the fields of child development, children's literature, and evaluation of pupil learning in reading.

The reading materials chosen for the children should take into account their general stage of reading development, interests, and desires. Therefore, each child chooses materials to read from among those available. A teacher using this program must provide materials with a wide range of difficulty, content, and format.

Teachers will confer with the children about what they have been reading and note progress in the records. If the teacher sees that there are several children having similar difficulties with their reading, a small group with common difficulties would be organized for instructional purposes.

The teacher will most likely arrange for a sharing time, during which pupils can talk with other members of the class about the books they have read and read aloud favorite portions.

There have been various modifications of this approach. Sometimes, because of lack of materials, teachers may use a basal series, adding individualized reading as a supplementary program. Some teachers use a basal reader but allow the good readers to read ahead as fast as they can and in any sequence they wish. Another modification is for children to use the same material in the same sequence and carry out the same assignments but move along the path at their own rates.

When the individualized reading program was first introduced, the teacher was supposed to work with a child in a one-to-one relationship. Children were supposed to choose their own books, work at their own pace, and learn the skills or reading in relation to what they were reading rather than in sequential order. Although some teachers may still follow this completely individualized program, many have modified the program to include some group instruction, which allows for more teacher-pupil contact. Many teachers help children choose their books, and most present reading skills in a sequential manner.

Whether individualized reading is practiced in its purest form or in a modified form, the one constant is the easy accessibility of a wide range of books based on the interests and reading levels of the students.

Some of the advantages of the individualized approach are:

1. The reading material can be drawn from the best of children's literature, rather than being limited to a set of textbooks.
2. It is possible to capitalize on the child's special interests and unique background of experiences.
3. The child can progress at an individual rate.
4. The child's available learning time can be fully utilized. There is no sitting and listening while different children struggle with oral reading.
5. The individual conference is personalized rather than mechanical; it provides an opportunity for the development of human traits and values which are unique in the individual and are fostered by personal interaction.

6. The individual conference has special appeal to children.
7. Children seem to develop more favorable attitudes toward reading under this approach, and so they usually read more books.

Some of the disadvantages of the individualized approach are:

1. Children may have difficulty selecting a book of the appropriate level to stimulate reading.
2. There are few opportunities to develop readiness for reading a new selection. Motivation, background information, and techniques for attacking new vocabulary are not specifically addressed.
3. Skills taught in other reading programs may be missed if the teacher using this approach is not highly competent.

THE BACK-TO-BASICS MOVEMENT

Since the mid-1970s, an educational movement in the United States frequently referred to as "back-to-basics" has put an increased emphasis on the teaching of reading, communication skills, and mathematics, especially in the elementary schools.

The back-to-basics movement grew from two causes: the discontent of many parents and legislators with some of the curriculum experiments of the 1960s, and the economic difficulties of the 1970s, which reduced school budgets and forced communities to examine their educational priorities carefully.

Supporters of this movement have used several research studies by federal agencies to defend their position. One of these, a four-year study by the United States Office of Education completed in 1975, revealed that one out of five Americans was either functionally illiterate or unable to read and write without difficulty. These findings supported a study by the National Institute of Education which was published a year later. The decline in scores of students on college entrance examinations added more energy to the movement.

If the back-to-basics movement has reached your state, your child's first-grade teacher may have a list of basic skills that children in the school will be expected to accomplish before they complete sixth grade. These so-called minimum competencies will have been established by the state, along with a series of tests administered periodically to determine how well the children are developing these skills.

Over two thirds of the states have adopted minimum competency skills. If your state is one of these, the competencies should be on file in your child's school. If you move from the state, you may want to have the minimum competency list included in your child's records folder for reference.

Below is a sample list of basic skills for grades one through six from the state of Virginia. Other states have similar lists. These skills are taught as children reveal a readiness for them.

1. The student will identify words encountered in written or oral form.
2. The student will use structural analysis and context clues to identify words.
3. The student will identify antonyms, synonyms, homonyms, and homographs and demonstrate a knowledge of their meanings.
4. The student will identify the main idea in a reading selection.
5. The student will arrange events in sequence from a reading selection.
6. The student will classify items or events.
7. The student will predict outcomes from a reading selection.
8. The student will locate and verify factual information on who, what, when, where, or why in a reading selection.
9. The student will distinguish fact, fiction, and opinion in a reading selection.
10. The student will determine cause-and-effect relationships.
11. The student will determine the meaning of words from context clues.
12. The student will follow oral or written directions.
13. The student will locate information.
14. The student will organize information.

SHOULD NONREADERS BE HELD BACK IN FIRST GRADE?

Children vary in their ability to learn words and to comprehend what they are reading. Some of them will have mastered the skills presented in first grade. Others may have mastered only a portion of the skills. These children will probably be placed in a second-grade class that is paced slower for reading instruction only. Or they may go to an average second-grade classroom and see a reading teacher for special reading instruction. Other children who may have problems in math and reading may need to repeat first grade.

The question to retain—that is, hold a student back—is not an easy one to answer. Some educators feel that retention is the best solution for children who have not mastered the reading or math skills.

Other educators do not feel that retention is the best solution. They suggest that children who have not mastered the first-grade skills be promoted to second grade and that the curriculum be adjusted to meet their needs.

The reason why a child has not learned the skills may be due to many reasons: immaturity, lack of background experiences, poor physical health, poor visual or auditory skills, or a combination of these. If your child is faced with retention, more than likely the school principal or teacher has warned you several months before the school year ends. Some principals will also personally talk to the children who will be retained. The children are told they have not been bad and they are not being punished. They just have not learned all the information they were expected to learn this year.

Some children are quite accepting, recognizing that they have not been consistent in completing assignments or understanding what was being taught. They know that they need more practice or time to learn the material. Others are not as accepting. They feel they are being given an unfair judgment. Your patience and understanding will be most important at this time. If you feel unsure about how to handle this situation, ask the principal of your school for some ideas. You may also want to ask the school psychologist for ways to handle this delicate situation.

THE IMPORTANCE OF VISION AND HEARING IN FIRST GRADE

Some students have vision or hearing defects which may hold them back in their progress in learning. It is important to find out about these problems and correct them as early as possible. Your pediatrician can refer you to other professionals, such as audiologists, opthalmologists, and optometrists. Also talk to your child's teacher to see if he or she has observed any visual or hearing problems in your child at school. For instance, does your child have difficulty seeing what is written on the blackboard? Does he or she complain of having headaches or sore eyes? Does he or she have trouble listening to or following directions? Does he or she have difficulty distinguishing between sounds? These are but a few examples of warning signs that may crop up in first grade.

Possible Symptoms of a Visual Problem

1. Rubs eyes when reading.
2. Needs to hold the book very close to eyes to read.
3. Squints.
4. Has difficulty copying from the blackboard. Makes lots of mistakes when copying.
5. Skips lines when reading. Unable to keep or find place.
6. Turns head at unusual angle to try to see better.
7. Has frequent headaches.
8. Holds hand over one eye to block it out.
9. Has watery, bloodshot eyes.
10. Is unable to continue reading very long.
11. Points to words while reading.
12. Has prescription glasses but never wears them.
13. Prefers to sit very close to TV screen.
14. Is inattentive when activity involves reading.
15. Has difficulty in tracing.

(From Miles V. Zintz, *Corrective Reading,* 4th ed. Dubuque, Ia.: W. C. Brown Co., 1981, p. 157. Reprinted by permission.)

Some of the common vision problems and symptoms are in the chart on the following page.

Common Vision Problems

TECHNICAL NAME	COMMON NAME	CONDITION	SYMPTOMS
Myopia	Nearsightedness	Clear vision at near point; blurring of distant images	Squinting at the board; holding print close to face; inattention to board work
Hyperopia	Farsightedness	Clear vision at far point; blurring of close objects	Holding print well away from face; disinterest in close work; eye fatigue during reading
Astigmatism		Distortion and/or blurring of part or all of visual field, far and near	Eye fatigue; headache; squinting; tilting or turning head; nausea during reading
Amblyopia	Lazy eye	Suppression of vision in one eye; dimming of vision without structural cause	Tilting or turning head to read; eye fatigue on one side; headache
Strabismus	Crossed eyes	Difficulty converging and focusing both eyes on the same object	Squinting; closing or covering one eye to focus; eye misaligning
Phoria or fusion problems; binocular coordination		Imbalance of ocular muscles; difficulty converging and focusing both eyes equally	Squinting; closing or covering one eye
Aniseikonia		Differences in size or shape of image in each eye	Blurring; squinting; difficulty focusing or fusing image; closing one eye

(From Jean Wallace Gillet and Charles Temple, *Understanding Reading Problems: Assessment and Instruction*. Boston: Little, Brown & Company, 1982. p. 306. Reprinted by permission.)

Hearing-impaired children have two different problems in receiving sound: loudness and distortion. Specialists typically define hearing problems either functionally or by the degree of loss.

A functional measure of hearing loss describes how a hearing-impaired person can use hearing for the ordinary purposes of life. According to this definition, a hearing-impaired person may be either deaf or hard of hearing.

- *Deaf.* When hearing is so impaired that it cannot be used for the ordinary purposes of life, with or without a hearing aid.
- *Hard of hearing.* When hearing is impaired but can be used for the ordinary purposes of life, with the use of a hearing aid. For a variety of reasons, some people who are hard of hearing do not use or benefit from a hearing aid.

When hearing is measured by degree of loss, hearing tests are used to determine how great a hearing loss has been suffered.

The audiometer measures the loudness of sound in a range of 0 to 110 decibels. These decibel levels serve as the basis for these categories of hearing impairment:

- Mildly hearing-impaired: loss between 20 and 40 decibels.
- Moderately hearing-impaired: loss between 40 and 70 decibels.
- Severely hearing-impaired: loss between 70 and 92 decibels.
- Profoundly hearing-impaired: loss greater than 92 decibels.

(U. S. Department of Health, Education, and Welfare, Head Start Project, *Mainstreaming Preschoolers: Children with Hearing Impairment.* Washington, D.C., 78-3116, 1978, p. 14.)

Possible Symptoms of a Hearing Loss

1. Fails to talk in appropriate tones (speech too loud).
2. Ignores comments (either negative or positive).
3. Constantly asks teacher or classmates to repeat.
4. Has difficulty learning and retaining (word sounds or spelling words).
5. Frequently picks or probes the ear.
6. Strains to hear: Tilts the head, cups hand behind ear, leans toward speaker, has stiff or restrained posture while listening.

7. Enunciates poorly.
8. Scores low on auditory discrimination or auditory memory tests.
9. Misses or misinterprets details in oral directions. Responds to written instructions better than to oral instructions.
10. Has physical evidence of ear problem: discharge, ringing sound.
11. Shows low attention span while oral activities are going on.
12. Has colds frequently: history of ear infections.
13. Tends to withdraw from peers and to play alone.
14. Tends to avoid listening-center activities.
15. Is easily distracted.
16. Complains of noise. Cannot concentrate in a noisy environment because of the confusion of many sounds.
17. Opens mouth while listening.
18. Watches the speaker closely, as if lip-reading.

(Miles V. Zintz, *Corrective Reading,* 4th ed. Dubuque, Ia.: W. C. Brown Co., 1981, p. 156. Reprinted by permission.)

WHAT CAN YOU DO TO HELP YOUR FIRST-GRADER?
The five basic activities that help develop successful readers should continue into your child's first year in school. Here are some specific suggestions for helpful activities you and your child will enjoy.

TALKING WITH AND LISTENING TO YOUR CHILD
Most first-graders want to share news about what they are learning at school. They will be proud of their artwork, their sentence or story accompanying a picture, the letters of the alphabet they can write, and the list of words they have learned to read. Listen attentively and encourage them to share their school experiences with you whenever you can—while fixing dinner, during after-school snacks, at the dinner table, before bedtime. If your child is the silent type, however, don't bombard him or her with such intimidating questions as, "What did you learn in school today?" Be low-key and encouraging instead.

In addition to listening attentively, look at your child's papers. Are the letters written properly, or are some reversed? It is not uncommon for children to reverse their letters at this grade level. If you observe reversals in numerals and letters, such as E for 3, S for 5, Υ for 7, P for 9, d for b, m for n, and 9 for q, ask your child to make the numerals or letters they appear to have difficulty with so that you can see how they form them. In most cases, showing the child how to form them properly solves the problem.

Perhaps you can purchase a tablet in the drugstore or variety store with the numerals 1 to 10 and the alphabet (upper- and lower-case letters) printed on it. Keeping this example available while your child is doing homework or independent activities will be very helpful.

Having the child trace over letters using the proper strokes is also helpful. This can be done by having the child trace an example on paper with crayon, or having the child trace letters in a small tray containing sand, salt, or chocolate pudding. This tactile experience is frequently used by first-grade teachers with children who have problems learning the correct formation of letters and numerals.

READING TO YOUR CHILD
(AND HAVING YOUR CHILD READ TO YOU)

As your children learn to read, they will want to read to you as well as be read to. This is a very important change in this basic activity and one that will be emphasized in the activities presented below.

Many teachers send specific activities to work on at home, such as activity sheets and game ideas, that are planned to reinforce activities in the formal reading program at school. Others recommend that parents continue to read aloud to children instead. In either case, the teachers will expect time to be set aside for your child to do homework related to the school reading program. The amount of time will depend on the teacher, but approximately thirty minutes is appropriate for most first-graders.

Activity 1:

There are various ways of talking about a story you have read to a child. They include:

- having your child tell the story to you or another adult.
- asking the child to tell you about the part of the story he or she liked best or the part he or she liked least.
- having the child draw a picture of his or her favorite or least favorite part of the story and dictating a sentence to tell you what the picture is about. (If the child can write a sentence, encourage him or her to do so.)
- having your child tell or write another ending to the story.

In this activity, if your child can't recall the sequence of events in the story, review it by turning the pages of the book and talking about what happened at the beginning, in the middle, and at the end, so that your child can identify his or her mistake. With practice, your child should be able to tell the story in sequence. Being able to tell a story in sequence is one of the objectives of many first-grade reading programs.

Activity 2:

First-grade teachers will often encourage parents to check out library books that are appropriate for the beginning reader. You may feel apprehensive about making a selection or having the child make a selection on his own. Here's a rule of thumb that really works: If your child looks at a page of print and finds five different words (one word per finger) that he or she doesn't know, the book is too difficult to read alone. At times when you are not able to take your child to the library but have time to pick up half a dozen books or more in the Easy Reading section, you can bring them home and apply this test to determine which ones the child can read on his or her own and which ones you will read together.

Activity 3:

If you cannot always be at home to read stories to your child, use your tape recorder, if you have one. One evening when you are reading a story to your child, especially one of his or her favorites, turn on the tape recorder. When you are away, the cassette can be played by the child. You'll be partially present through your familiar voice. As the child listens to your taped version, he or she can follow along by turning the pages of the book or reading silently while listening.

Activity 4:

Another use of the tape recorder is to have your child record a story while reading it to you. Your child can then play it back and enjoy listening to the story when you are not able to be there. There are many advantages to having children record their own voices. They can listen to themselves and have the pleasure of enjoying their unique voices; they can enjoy stories by their favorite authors that have had to be returned to the library; they can maintain a record of how well they are progressing in their oral skills. They may even want to share the tape with a relative to show off how well they are doing in reading.

If your child is a word-by-word oral reader, don't be concerned. Many first-graders are choppy readers, but as they gain more confidence and skill through practice at school and home, they become more fluent. Smooth oral reading comes only through practice.

Activity 5:

As children gain greater proficiency in reading, they will want to do more reading than listening. You can still use your time with them to reinforce some of the skills being introduced by their teacher. After your child has read a story to you, turn to a page and do the following:

- Say a word that ends like a word on that page and ask the child to find and read the word with the same ending.
- Say a word that rhymes with a word on that page and ask the child to find the word that rhymes.
- Ask the child to find all the words on that page that begin with a given consonant sound. Follow with one or two others as time permits. You can find the materials from school to determine which consonant sounds have been introduced.

If you wonder whether your child has memorized the story

he or she is reading aloud to you, point to a sentence, read half of it to your child, and then ask him or her to finish it. Or ask your child a question that will require him or her to read a specific sentence to answer it.

Activity 6:

Keep a joke or riddle book handy in the kitchen or family room. When you feel in the mood for a good laugh, ask your child to read a riddle or a joke to you. Some of these books are listed in Appendix A. This will help your child to enjoy humorous writing. After doing this several times, you may ask your child to *tell* the riddle or joke rather than read it. This will make it part of his or her own joke or riddle repertoire, which first-graders begin to build.

BEING A READING MODEL FOR YOUR CHILD

First-grade children are eager to learn from the adults around them. In the earlier chapters you have read about ways to show that reading is an integral part of your life. Continue to be an example for your child.

Activity 1:

Initiate a program at home where at least once a week for ten or fifteen minutes *everyone* in the house or apartment stops what they are doing and reads for pleasure. One family we know set aside Sunday morning for reading, probably the least hectic time of the week for many families. If it is not possible for the whole family to do this together, one parent and one child might initiate the program and read independently at the same time. You may want to begin this program by reading the newspapers together and then let your child select other types of reading materials.

Activity 2:

Introduce your child to a hobby such as coin or stamp collecting. He or she can find books in the public or school library that will discuss how to begin a collection. You may have a hobby of your own that you would like to introduce to your child; perhaps there are books written about the hobby that you can read together.

Your child may be in Scouting and may learn how to make some arts and crafts projects. If he or she shows an interest in learning more about the activity, use this as another way to demonstrate the importance of reading directions on how to assemble something.

Activity 3:

Children like to learn more about information they heard or saw on radio or television or read about in school. Now is the time to introduce them to primary dictionaries and reference books. You do not have to purchase them for your own home. Public libraries have them, as well as most school libraries. Some first-graders are more curious than others and will enjoy looking through reference books or using them. Others who have older brothers or sisters will try to imitate the older children. Do not force your child to look through or use these materials if he or she shows no interest in them. As your child progresses in school, he or she will be introduced to them later.

Activity 4:

First-graders sometimes want to help prepare snacks or part of the evening meal. While you may not have a lot of patience or time because of your schedule, you may want to find some easy-to-follow recipes your child can make. There are a variety of children's cookbooks on the library shelves that you can try before purchasing one for your child. Some grocery stores distribute one-page flyers that give simple recipes you and your child could try whenever your schedule permits.

Activity 5:

If your home is typical, the television set is in high demand at times. One way to settle family arguments is to check the TV section of the newspaper and plan a schedule that will satisfy a majority of the family. Do not expect your first-grader to be able to read the TV section on his or her own, but point out how to find some of his or her favorite programs. Show your child how to find a program on a specific page or in a specific column by finding one of your favorites first.

GOING PLACES WITH YOUR CHILD

Your first-grader will probably be better company than he or she was as an infant or toddler. A six-year-old begins conversations with relative ease. Some parents are quite surprised to hear their child recall details about past family activities, including many details that the parents may have forgotten. A six-year-old child loves to suggest choices for a weekend activity.

Activity 1:

Many first-graders enjoy revisiting places they have seen before. For example, you may have taken your child to a museum or historic site. The first time you were there, he or she may have noticed only the pretty flowers in a certain room or watched a film. The second visit may be more exciting for your child than the first, because he or she notices more things. Your child may even try to read some of the plaques or signs posted around the building or on the grounds.

Trips to the zoo, the local airport, the park, or the lake continue to provide enjoyment for first-graders. Your child may relate something he or she heard in school or read about in a storybook to the current experience. For instance, in a story that your child heard at school, there were benches in the park. Your child may notice that your local park has similar benches and tell you about it.

Activity 2:

You may want to take advantage of some of the free tours available in your community. For example, many fire stations and police stations have an annual open house. Take your child to the open house and later discuss some of the things you saw and enjoyed. Local newspapers often list such free or special events. When you can, participate in these events with your child. He or she will learn more about the community you live in, and these experiences will help him or her to understand the stories found in schoolbooks.

Activity 3:

While doing routine chores, such as driving, ask your child to help you recall or locate some landmarks en route to your destination. For example, as you drive to school, discuss what familiar landmarks help you to get to the school. Through this activity you can help your child learn directions (left and right), learn to use his or her visual memory (recalling what will be coming up in the next block or two), and learn to refine his or her visual-discrimination skills by identifying the kinds of houses or trees that appear along the way.

Activity 4:

Trips to the mountains or an amusement park are enjoyable for six-year-old children. Encourage your child to pay attention to the different kinds of sounds you can hear while walking about. This encourages the child to distinguish between familiar and unfamiliar noises, such as the sounds of laughter, the pitch of voices, the sounds of the birds and other animals, the sounds that different machines make, and the sounds of footsteps on the pavement. While your child is in school, he or she may recall these sounds while listening to the teacher read a story or while viewing a movie or filmstrip.

Ask your child to try to recall some of the sounds that he or she once heard while you were together at home or while walking or riding in the car. This will give you a picture of his or her auditory memory skills. Do not use this activity as a monotonous drill; keep it playful and fun.

Activity 5:

During first grade, children learn that the library houses a variety of books with different purposes. There are books that are purely imaginative, created by the author primarily to entertain the reader (fiction). There are books that are completely factual, written primarily to inform or give advice (nonfiction). There are books about people, sometimes written by others (biography) and sometimes written by themselves (autobiography). As you enter the world of children's literature, you may renew your acquaintance with old friends through the books that your child brings home, or make new friends with a host of delightful characters.

There are so many new books for children published each year, it is difficult even for those who specialize in this field to keep up. You certainly don't need to do that to be a good parent. You can rely on the children's librarian in your public library. This person is usually professionally trained for the position and is very familiar with the collection of books that the library has.

There are also book clubs for children. The biggest advantage of book clubs for children is that the books received are yours. You may read them over and over again and share them with friends. If you don't want to enroll your child in a book club because of the expense involved, from time to time try to purchase books as gifts. Although some children's books are expensive, they are not as expensive as many toys that break or become boring easily. There are also inexpensive paperback editions of many of the best books, and these are often found in grocery stores and drugstores as well as at garage sales, library book sales, bazaars, flea markets, and book fairs at schools. It's important, we believe, for children to have books of their own.

INVOLVING YOUR CHILD IN A VARIETY OF RECREATIONAL ACTIVITIES

Activity 1:

Frequently first-graders are very interested in writing, and you may want to encourage your child's interest in writing and spelling by playing word games.

Take the time to play word games such as Hangman, Dr. Spello, Boggle, Split Words, and so on with your child. You may want to share one of the favorite games you recall playing when you were a child.

Activity 2:

Introduce your child to a sport that you like and would like your child to participate in with you: tennis, racquetball, soccer, skiing, or fishing. As you introduce your child to this sport, talk about the necessary safety precautions and the techniques used in the sport. Talk about your experiences together and how it feels to participate in the sport for the first time. You may want to take pictures of this experience. Once the pictures are developed, you can suggest that your child write a sentence or two about the new activity. Your child may even want to talk about it during the next show-and-tell time at school. This can encourage your child to recall facts or a sequence of events and use his or her visual memory while talking about the sport.

Activity 3:
Some first-graders show an interest in doing simple crossword puzzles. You may want to try the ones in children's magazines. You can always try to do the crossword puzzles found in the comics section of the newspapers.

Activity 4:
You may want to take your child to see a basketball, baseball, soccer, or football game. Once you arrive at home, you can talk about the game and show him or her how to keep up with the record the team has thus far in the season. The sports page of the newspaper will become interesting to the child, even if he or she only looks at the pictures initially.

Activity 5:
Some children enjoy painting or doing arts and crafts. Check your newspapers or community flyers for special classes planned for six-year-olds. These activities help a child express his or her creativity and require the child to use eye-hand motor-control skills.

Whenever you plan to enroll your child in a special class, take the time to observe the class. Many first-graders cannot work on a specific task for a prolonged period of time. You will want to be sure this activity is pleasurable, not a chore or something to dread. In short, use common sense when selecting a class. Talk to the teacher if you have doubts about your child's participation.

6

QUESTIONS COMMONLY ASKED BY PARENTS

Parents often ask questions about reading and their children. We've tried to answer many of these questions in the earlier chapters of this book, but in this final chapter we'll try to address some specific concerns we could not cover elsewhere.

Question: I'm expecting my first child in a few months and would like to be an effective parent. Are there any parent associations I can join to help me?

Answer: There are several national organizations designed to help their members become more effective parents. Their names and addresses are listed in Appendix D. These organizations have magazines and newsletters paid for by one's membership fee. There are organizations for single parents, as well as for those with exceptional children. Many also have local branches. Check the yellow pages of your phone directory under "Organizations" to see if there are any local branches of these groups in your area; you may want to consider joining one. If you are anxious to meet with other parents to talk about topics and problems of mutual interest, you might organize a small group in your neighborhood, or at your church. A small group of parents available to talk about the ups and downs of parenthood can be a very valuable support for any parent.

Question: What can I do with a very bright preschooler who is bored by the nursery school I selected?

Answer: As mentioned in Chapter 3, nursery-school programs vary tremendously. The more traditional programs place a heavy emphasis on the child's social, emotional, and physical development and less emphasis on the child's intellectual development. Others place a heavy emphasis on the child's intellectual development.

The nursery-school program you selected may be one that places less emphasis on the intellectual development of children. Because of this, your child appears bored by the activities. If your child is so turned off by the nursery school that you and your child are upset, you may want to investigate nursery-school programs that place a greater emphasis on your child's intellectual growth.

Nursery-school programs that use the system developed by Maria Montessori, an Italian doctor and educator, have become very popular in recent years in the United States. Many parents of very bright children who were not stimulated by more traditional nursery schools tell us that their children responded positively to the methods used in Montessori schools. Parents wishing to learn more about the Montessori system should write to the American Montessori Society, 175 Fifth Avenue, New York, New York 10010.

Question: My eight-year-old son has average-to-above-average intelligence, but he has a very negative attitude about reading. What can be done?

Answer: This is a very difficult question to answer without knowing what might have caused this negative attitude and how negative the attitude really is. It could be that your son prefers other activities to reading but enjoys the things he does read. A lot of boys are turned off by formal reading in school for several reasons. First of all, they often mature more slowly than girls and thus are often less successful in beginning programs than girls. Second, the content of some basal reading series is not as exciting as the lives of many of the children who read them. That's why they find the books boring and develop a negative attitude toward all books. Finally, there is a lot of pressure on young children to read well, and a lot of school time is devoted to this activity. You can probably see how a child might develop a negative attitude if a lot of time is spent on one activity when the child would prefer doing something else.

There are some things, however, that you may want to try at home to help your child develop a more positive attitude toward reading:

1. Talk with him about his current interests and then check out books related to them at the public library.
2. Find out what he enjoys reading most and help him set aside time outside of school to read the kinds of materials he likes. Even if he prefers books of jokes, riddles, magic tricks, or even comic books, he is having a pleasurable reading experience, and you are recognizing the fact that these reading materials are acceptable as well.
3. When local authors visit the library or his school, encourage your child to check out books by the author he has met. Some children are very interested in reading a book by a real author with whom they have actually talked.
4. Sometimes children think that the only reason for learning to read is to be able to read at school. You can help your son better understand the importance of reading by involving him in functional reading at home. For example, he can help read recipes, directions to games, instructions for putting toys together, and other similar types of materials that should have real meaning to him.
5. Purchase books for yourself as well as for your son. A personal collection of books permits one to read and reread books by a favorite author, or books on a particular topic.
6. Watch a television special on a topic your son likes and then read books related to the topic. For instance, a Jacques Cousteau television special could spark interest in marine biology books or books written by Jacques Cousteau himself.
7. Finally, encourage your eight-year-old to keep a journal of the exciting things he does each week and then to read his book of adventures to members of his family. Most young children like to write about themselves and by becoming authors themselves have a greater interest in what others have written.

Question: My child is having difficulty reading. The teacher has suggested that he has dyslexia or a learning disability.

What do the terms mean, and what can I do to help my child?
Answer: The terms learning disability and dyslexia identify students with average or above-average intelligence who are having problems learning to read.

Generally speaking, a learning disability is a discrepancy between a student's actual and expected achievement in math, reading, spoken or written language, and spatial orientation. A more precise and technical definition is "a generic term that refers to a heterogenous group of disorders manifested by significant difficulties in the acquisition and use of listening, speaking, reading, writing, or mathematical abilities. Even though a learning disability may occur concomitantly with other handicapping conditions (for example, sensory impairment, mental retardation, social and emotional disturbance) or environmental influence (for example, cultural difference, insufficient/inappropriate instruction, psychogenic factors), it is not the direct result of those conditions or influences."

Generally speaking, dyslexia describes a student who is unable to learn to read despite conventional classroom experience. This term is applied when a professional suspects that there is a central nervous system dysfunction. Technically speaking, dyslexia is "a medical term for incomplete alexia; partial, but severe, inability to read; historically (but less common in current use) word blindness. Dyslexia is a rare but definable and diagnosable form of primary reading retardation with some form of central nervous system dysfunction. It is not attributable to environmental causes or other handicapping conditions."

Ask the teacher to cite his or her reasons for suspecting that your child has dyslexia or a learning disability. The reason should be specific—for example, your child reads words backward or reverses letters. Ask that your child be tested to determine the problem. The learning-disabilities teacher, the school psychologist, or the reading teacher can administer tests to aid you in learning more about your child's strengths and weaknesses. If necessary, request a parental conference with the school principal and the classroom teacher to initiate the testing. Additionally, you may seek help outside, such as educational or psychological testing services at a college, university, or private testing center. Regardless of where the testing is done, it may take quite a while to set up an appointment. Suggest that the teacher refrain from labeling your child as a dyslexic until the results are known.

Question: What kind of success in reading can I expect for my Down's syndrome child?
Answer: Much has been done within the past ten years in the area of teaching Down's syndrome children. Medical and educational researchers have found that Down's syndrome children vary in their intellectual and motor ability. It is difficult to project success without more definitive information concerning the child, such as developmental and educational or academic testing would reveal. Once such information is known, a reading program can be planned. There are special-education specialists within most school systems who are trained to work with Down's syndrome children and their parents. For further information, contact the Down's Syndrome Congress, 20438 Renfrew Road, Detroit, MI 48221 or the National Association for Retarded Citizens, 2709 Avenue E East, Arlington, TX 76011.

Question: During a recent parent-teacher conference, my child's first-grade teacher said that my child skips over words and doesn't follow a line of print. She suggested that he do eye exercises. What do you think?
Answer: The value of eye exercises is controversial. But first, has someone determined that your son has a vision problem? If so, who and by what means? School vision screening isn't always accurate, so it should be followed by a professional eye examination. Consult your pediatrician or the American Optometric Association, 243 North Lindbergh Boulevard, St. Louis, MO 63141 for specifics. Many people go to an ophthalmologist, while others go to an optometrist for eye testing. If you get an opinion that varies from what you feel may be the real problem, seek a second opinion. Ophthalmologists typically do not recommend eye exercises; some optometrists do, however.

Question: My child's teacher has suggested that I get a private tutor to help my child with phonics and grammar. What suggestions do you have for selecting a private tutor for my primary-age child?

Answer: Parents need to determine (1) the subject matter the child appears to need help in and (2) how outside help could be beneficial. If your child is having difficulty in English, reading, or language arts, you could employ a teacher who specializes in the specific area, or a college student majoring in the specific area. One can also turn to private tutoring ads that appear in the newspaper or the phone directory. Private tutoring can be done by a company that employs tutors, or by an individual running a small tutoring business. If your child has specific problems that have been diagnosed, you may want a tutor with a more specific background. When you contact individuals working as tutors, ask specific questions about their qualifications, where the tutoring will take place, the time of each session, and the duration of the tutorial program. Inquire about progress reports, and be sure that the child and tutor have a good rapport. After all, you are seeking help for your child, and attitude is important.

Question: I have never been a good reader, and I wonder if my child will have the same problems I had. Are reading problems inherited?

Answer: There appears to be no evidence that reading problems are inherited. Some physical problems, however, can have an effect on reading. For example, a visual problem, such as an astigmatism, may be found in both a parent and a child. Since research indicates that there is no single cause for reading problems, reading specialists continue to diagnose each child individually for his or her strengths and weaknesses in the reading process. If you are concerned about the possibility of your child having reading problems, check with his or her teachers or have the child's reading ability tested.

Question: I'm afraid my first-grade child has a hearing problem. I tell her to do something and she doesn't do it until I tell her again. How can I determine whether she is hard of hearing or just lazy?

Answer: If you really believe your daughter has a hearing problem, you may see evidence of this other than the fact that she does not follow your directions. Does she always try to face people when they are talking to her? Does she turn up the TV or record player louder than normal? Does she turn one ear toward the person speaking to her? These are a few signs that she may have a hearing problem. Have her ears examined by an audiologist or at a speech and hearing clinic, which usually charges a nominal fee.

If your daughter does not have a hearing problem, however, she may just not fully understand what you are saying to her and fail to respond because of her lack of comprehension. We cannot assume that everything we say to a young child has meaning to them. Primary-school-age children may hear your words but not interpret them in the way you do. It's not that they are lazy, it's just that they are children; their brains are in a stage of development that is appropriate for them, but different from that of adults. You may need to repeat your request using different words or focusing the child's attention on the activity by demonstrating what you want done. A lot of patience is required. Ask your daughter's teacher to observe whether your daughter continues to have a problem following directions. If she does, educational testing can be done through the school system.

Question: As a working parent of three children, how can I give my younger children the same kind of attention I gave my firstborn to help them enjoy reading?
Answer: Parents often feel that they were better parents to their first child than to any of the others because they usually spent more time reading and playing with the first child than with the other children. Firstborn children usually receive a great deal of attention from their parents; when another child comes into the family, one's time must be divided and the second child may receive less attention than the first did. Although you may feel guilty about it, you really should not. The evidence suggests that the amount of time one spends with children is less important than the way in which that time is used. Some of the ideas in this book may help you to make better use of the limited amount of time you have to spend with your younger children. You must also remember,

too, that although you may not be able to give your second or third child as much attention as you would like, the child is receiving lots of attention from the other children in the family rather than only from the parents.

If you feel guilty because some of your younger children are not reading as well as your firstborn, realize that there is no certainty that spending more time with your children makes them better readers. What you do with the time, however, does make a difference.

Question: I think the reading program in my child's school is terrible. What can I do about it?

Answer: When you describe your child's reading program as "terrible," it's hard to know exactly what you do not like. It may just be different from the one that you used when you were in school, or it may be truly ineffective.

If the reading program is just different from the one used when you were learning to read, that is to be expected. Educators make use of current research and experience to improve their practices, and so schools should always be changing to reflect the progress of the profession. New methods and materials are generally accepted in other professions, but some adults seem to find them upsetting in the public schools.

If your child's reading program is ineffective, then you have a legitimate reason to complain about it. No matter how modern and well tested a program might be, if it is not working for your child, then another program should be provided as an alternative. Just like the members of any other profession, educators should be accountable to those for whom they provide services. If you are dissatisfied with your child's reading program, talk with your child's teacher immediately to find out why the program is not working and what can be done about it. Naturally, if the teacher is unable to provide you with the answers to these questions, the principal or the reading specialist of the school should be contacted.

Question: My son scores well on achievement tests yet is not doing well in reading. What should I do?

Answer: Many students score well on standardized tests because of the test format, which provides them with several possible answers. The student merely selects one answer based on the information presented in the question. If your son scores well on the reading section of the achievement tests, you may want to talk to his classroom teacher or reading teacher. Ask whether they have observed his reading. He may be the type of child who does well on multiple-choice tests by guessing at the answers but does not do well when he has to write out an answer in essay form.

If he has a negative attitude toward reading, he may not be using his reading ability for his regular schoolwork. It takes a positive attitude toward learning to seek out answers to questions within a textbook chapter as compared to selecting one out of several answers conveniently listed on a standardized test. If his reading skills are good, then you need to find ways to change his attitude toward reading. The family can establish a half-hour reading period when everyone must do some kind of reading—comic books, humorous books, books that deal with a TV series, or a series by a specific author. Perhaps several family members can read the same book and discuss it. Parents are important reading models for their children, as we've stressed throughout this book.

Question: As a parent of a fourth-grader, I was very surprised at the test results I received from the school system. I got percentile scores to report my daughter's progress. A few years ago, my sister's children were in the elementary grades, and she got grade-level scores on the results of her children's tests. Why was I not given grade-level scores?

Answer: Many school systems now report the results of achievement tests in percentile scores instead of grade-level scores. The percentile score describes where your child's score stands in relation to the sample of children tested when the test was developed. This means, for example, that if your child's score was at the 76th percentile, she did as well as or better than 76 percent of the students in the sample. It also means that 24 percent did better than your child.

The grade-level score means that a student scored as well as a typical student in a certain grade and a certain month, not that the student should be in that grade. For example, if your daughter scored 3.6 on her reading achievement test, her score means that she did as well as an average third-grader in the sixth month of school on this test. It does not mean that she should be in the sixth month of third grade or doing third-grade work.

Write to the Consumer Information Center, Department 520J, Pueblo, CO 81009 for a free publication entitled *Your Child and Testing* by Enid B. Herndon; it is produced by the National Institute of Education. The Association of American Publishers, 1 Park Avenue, New York, NY 10016 has a free publication entitled *Standardized Testing*. To receive it, send a No. 10 self-addressed stamped envelope.

Question: I am a parent with four children ranging in ages from seven to sixteen. It seems to me that my youngest is being tested more than my oldest was when she was in elementary school. Why are children given so many tests? Are these tests really needed?

Answer: Most state departments of education and county school divisions require that all children be tested several times during their years in school. The exact type and number of tests given vary with each state. The purpose of testing is to improve the instruction and learning of students. There are two major types of tests given to students. They are norm-referenced achievement tests and criterion-referenced tests. Students in elementary school (kindergarten to sixth grade) typically get achievement tests.

These tests are all norm-referenced, which means that numerical scores are assigned to each grade level. This enables a child's performance to be measured against those of all other children taking the test at the child's age level when the test was developed and the norms established.

Achievement tests measure how much students have learned in social studies, science, reading, English/language arts, and math. It tells the school personnel how well your child has done in comparison to students who were in the norming sample and can tell how well the students in the class have done when compared with other classes within the school district, county, state, or nation.

The most recent form of tests are criterion-referenced tests, which are designed to measure knowledge and abilities against certain specified behavioral objectives. School systems are using criterion-referenced tests because the tests can be tailor-made for any grade level and for any of the content areas (math, science, reading, etc.). These tests provide a way of measuring children's abilities without comparing the children to a norm group.

Question: My four-year-old son knows his alphabet and can count to twenty by himself. Does this mean he will do well in kindergarten and score well on a reading-readiness test?

Answer: Many nursery-school-age children can recite the ABC's and successfully count to ten or twenty. Your son may have learned these skills by watching *Sesame Street,* looking at picture and number books, playing with children in the neighborhood or in a nursery school, or by your talking and reading to him. Although both of you should feel good that he has learned how to say his alphabet and can count, this does not assure him of an easy experience in school. There may be others in kindergarten who can write the letters of the alphabet or who have already learned to read on their own.

Prior to the popularity of *Sesame Street,* knowledge of the alphabet was considered a good indicator of school success in beginning reading. Presently, less emphasis is placed on its value as a predictor of success in school.

Question: What can I do with a bright six-year-old boy who is very interested in school but seems bored in the evenings or on weekends at home?

Answer: Take time to talk to your child and point out some possible activities to do around the home or neighborhood in the evenings or on weekends. For example, does your child have a hobby or belong to a group? You could list the alternatives that are available to him and then let him select an activity or activities that appeal to him. If there are no children in the neighborhood, you will have to provide visits to parks or friends' homes for companionship and the opportunity to play games.

You may want to check your local newspapers for weekend events or look in the phone directory for parent groups which would give you more ideas.

You may also want to enroll your child in an arts and crafts course in your community or a workshop offered at the "Y." These could provide your child with some of the same structures he enjoys in school, yet offer a change from academic subjects. Whatever you do, don't overplan your child's free time.

Question: My child is seven years old and repeating first grade. He is above average in intelligence, has a mild auditory memory problem, and desperately wants to learn to read. I want to help him but can't spend hours working with him each evening because of other responsibilities. What can I do to help him learn to read?

Answer: If your son has been diagnosed as a learning-disabled child, ask the learning-disability-resources teacher to give you ideas in addition to these:

1. Play "Simon Says" with your son once a week, or ask the sitter or another adult to do it. You would say: "We will stand, and when I tell you something you will either follow the directions or just stand still. For example, if I say, 'Simon says touch your toes and touch your stomach,' you would touch your toes and then touch your stomach. However, if I say, 'Do a deep-knee bend,' you would stand still because I didn't say 'Simon says.' "

   You will want to begin with one- or two-step directions. Then you can request that your son follow three-step directions. You can also vary the game by asking him to sit and use his thumbs. For example, tell your son to put his thumbs up if what you say is correct and down if it's wrong. Examples: "Simon says *book* and *look* end the same way." Thumbs up. "Simon says *take* and *shake* begin with the same sound." Thumbs down. Perhaps the classroom teacher could give you help in selecting words to use.

2. If you are looking for a gift for your son, you may want to buy an electronic game such as Simon (Milton Bradley) or Merlin (Parker Brothers). The games require a player to repeat patterns that are heard.

3. If you have time in the car with your son, ask him to play a game with you. Talk about things you see and ask him to recall two to four things. As he becomes proficient at recalling up to four items, slowly increase the number of items. If you do not have the opportunity to drive around in a car with your son, you may greet him every evening at a specific time. Plan on taking time two or three times a week to get his attention and ask him to follow directions. Begin with simple directions and slowly increase the number of directions that he has to follow. Should you have limited time, ask the sitter or another adult to try these activities with him.

4. Inquire about the Talking Books program (Division for the Blind and Physically Handicapped), Library of Congress, Washington, DC 20542. There are regional and subregional libraries in most states that participate in this program. Your son can receive records or tapes of books that he can listen to. This eliminates the need for you to read to him all the time but permits him to hear stories and to learn to read along with the tape or record. You can still plan to read to him once a week or as often as you can.

Question: My twin children have been in special-education classes for two years now and will be mainstreamed for third grade. What can I do to help them prepare for their new setting?

Answer: Hopefully, your children's special-education teacher has spoken to you as well as to your children about the move. The teacher should help to prepare them. The children should know that their problem or difficulty in learning has improved to the point where they no longer need all the individualized help they were receiving. In other words, they have made progress and can do well in a regular classroom setting.

You can help your children to make the change with ease by talking about what they can expect in a regular classroom and by discussing any fears or apprehensions they may have. You may even want to request permission to visit a third-grade classroom with your children. Perhaps, if there is no change in buildings or principals, you may want to point out all the familiar aspects of the new situation. The visit will encourage the children as they observe similar books being used in the regular classroom, or that the teacher uses a similar method for lining up to go to the cafeteria. If there will be obvious changes you may want to point out these changes to your children at a slower pace. For example, request additional permission to visit a new school sometime during the summer when the building is open. Learning how to get to the rest rooms and cafeteria may ease some of the children's fears about the unknown.

Question: My three-year-old doesn't talk very much. She understands what is said to her and can carry out a request given by an adult. What can my wife and I do to encourage her to talk more?

Answer: There are several things you can do. First, if she has not had any speech or hearing testing, check with either the public-health services office in your county or your pediatrician to see what type of testing is available. In most communities there are services for preschool screenings for speech, hearing, and vision. This early testing will give you a more accurate picture of her current skills as well as ideas for activities you could do at home to improve her skills. Second, you may deliberately want *not* to do something your daughter has asked you to do by hand gestures. Instead, ask her to *tell* you what she wants before you comply with her request. Third, you may want to purchase the Learning Language at Home Kit by Merle B. Karnes. This kit has many activities specifically designed for parental use to develop children's language skills. It is published by the Council for Exceptional Children and can be purchased in teacher stores. Fourth, if your child does not have many playmates or is the eldest child, you may want to place her in a nursery school. Being with others her own age may encourage her to do more talking, since she will have to cope and cooperate with others. Of necessity she will have to make her wishes known or be an unwilling partner in an activity. Finally, read books such as *Emerging Language* 2 by John Hatten, Tracy Goman, and Carole Lent (Communication Skill Builders, Inc., Tucson, Az.: 1976) for activities to encourage children to communicate.

Question: One of the foster parents in the neighborhood talks about the foster child's reading problem and the IEP he has in his school. Just what is an IEP?

Answer: Your neighbor is caring for a foster child who has been tested and has special needs. The term IEP stands for Individualized Educational Program and is the result of a requirement of federal law PL 94-142, the Education of All Handicapped Children Act. There were several steps that took place prior to the child's participation in an IEP. These are (1) assessment (standardized and informal tests used to pinpoint the child's strengths and weaknesses in learning), (2) setting of long-range and short-term objectives necessary for the child to become a successful learner, (3) choice of instructional materials, procedures, and settings, and (4) an evaluation of the effort (annual and triannual posttesting that evaluates the child's progress).

Question: From time to time I read about special diets for children who have a learning disability or hyperactivity. Just what is all the fuss about?

Answer: Special-education and medical researchers have found that certain foods do affect the behaviors of some children. For example, sugar, milk, chocolate, wheat, apples, beef, chicken, and color additives and flavors (red food coloring) are just a few foods that have been identified as causes of allergic reactions, hives, hyperactivity, or depression in children. If parents are concerned about their child and a possible allergy problem, they should consult a pediatrician about an allergist for a diagnostic workup. In addition to the professional diagnosis, a parent can consult *The Journal of Learning Disabilities* or two books written by Dr. Benjamin Feingold entitled *Introduction to Clinical Allergy* and *Why Your Child is Hyperactive,* or attend lectures sponsored by many community agencies or colleges that deal with food allergies and learning problems. There are still no definite answers to the question about food allergies and the learning process.

Question: Will there be continuity in my daughter's reading program during the primary grades?

Answer: Yes. Assuming that your daughter stays in the same school system she will continue to learn more of the reading skills begun in first grade. Regardless of the program (basal, language experience, or individualized), your daughter will review, refine, and build her word-recognition and comprehension skills. Your daughter's classroom teacher, principal, or reading teacher can give you more of the specifics regarding the sequence of the skills for each grade level. Additionally, in some schools the Parent-Teacher Association has an annual meeting devoted to the reading program used at the school.

Generally speaking, the children will read materials that are increasingly lengthy and will read in a variety of content areas, such as math, science, health, and English. Of course, each subject has a special vocabulary, which the children are expected to understand.

To help a student successfully decode words and increase his or her knowledge of words, the third-grader is taught the basic dictionary skills: alphabetizing, syllabication, use of guide words and pronunciation key, pronunciation respelling, and definitions. These are further refined in fourth grade and beyond. Your child will also be expected to do book reports. In most instances she will be expected to convey what she liked or didn't like about the book. You may want to encourage her to read a variety of types of books. Third-graders tend to read books in a single subject area. Some teachers discourage this, because the student is not discovering all the types of children's literature available; for example, some students will read only animal stories and not venture into the areas of mysteries or autobiographies. Encourage your child to read widely so that she will not be told, "Karen, I don't want to read another nature story book report . . . you've done that for three months in a row." If necessary, use a TV special as an incentive to read a new book. All this is preparation for fourth grade, where greater emphasis is placed on the content.

Question: My six-year-old child had difficulty learning to read this year in first grade. Will there be some type of remedial program for my child if he is not reading by the end of the primary grades?

Answer: Yes. Most children who have a problem in first grade are able to read by second or third grade if their teachers are aware of the problem and attend to it. The sooner the child can receive additional help, the better it is for the child. A child's self-concept may suffer because of an inability to read as well as his or her peers.

There are many reasons why some children are not reading by the end of the third grade. Some may have received poor instruction; others may have visual, auditory, or speech problems that were undetected until first or second grade; some may have moved frequently or missed school too often; and still others may have other learning problems which need special attention and have not been attended to. There is no ready explanation why some children need more practice with each skill, while others grasp skills quickly.

Ask that the personnel at your child's school assess his strengths and weaknesses in reading. This will be done through a variety of standardized, informal, and criterion-referenced tests. Once your child's reading ability is determined, an instructional program will be provided. The amount of special instruction will depend upon the type of service offered in your school system. For example, your child may go to the reading teacher for a special reading class once, twice, or three days a week for a half-hour or hour class.

Question: My six-year-old will soon be in first grade. English is his second language. How will he be taught to read?

Answer: Many schools have specially trained teachers who teach English as a Second Language (ESL) classes. More than likely your son will first have opportunities to learn about the English language and will learn to speak English prior to receiving formal instruction in reading. Depending upon the school's choice, he then will learn to read in one of the types of programs described in Chapter 5 (basal, language experience, or individualized). It is common to see bilingual children using the linguistic basal program or the language experience program to meet their specific needs.

If you are fortunate, the school system in your area provides bilingual classes. Specially trained teachers would teach your son to read first in his native language and then in English.

The best method for teaching reading to bilingual children is a topic of controversy. No one method works best for all children. If you want more information, contact the ESL or bilingual curriculum specialist in your son's future school, or the local parent association or groups within your community. You can also call the National Clearinghouse for Bilingual Education in Roslyn, Virginia, at 1-800-336-4560 (toll-free) or 703-522-0710.

Question: Once my child begins reading on her own, will I still have a role to play in her learning experiences?
Answer: Definitely! Your child will continue to need reading role models and will need to continue learning more of the reading skills. You can encourage her to learn more about reading in a variety of ways: playing games like Scrabble, Boggle, and Hangman; working crossword puzzles in newspapers, children's magazines, or crossword puzzle books; following directions while cooking, baking, or making arts-and-crafts projects; and reading newspapers.

Your child may want to share her success in reading by reading jokes or riddles to family members and other adults. She may even ask to take turns when reading a bedtime story. Don't drill or quiz your child about her daily reading activities; instead, show interest by providing time for her to talk freely about it.

APPENDIX A
SOME FAVORITE BOOKS FOR CHILDREN

Picture Books (for Children Under Six)

Aitken, Amy. *Ruby.* Scarsdale, N.Y.: Bradbury Press, 1979. Ages 3–6.

Alexander, Martha. *Nobody Asked Me if I Wanted a Baby Sister,* illustrated by author. New York: Dial Press, 1971. Ages 5–7.

Anderson, C. W. *Billy and Blaze,* illustrated by author. New York: Macmillan, 1962. Ages 5–8.

———. *Blaze and Thunderbolt,* illustrated by author. New York: Macmillan, 1955. Ages 5–8.

Ardizzone, Edward. *Little Tim and The Brave Sea Captain,* illustrated by author. New York: Walck, 1970. Ages 5–8.

Arnstein, Helene. *Billy and Our New Baby.* New York: Human Sciences Press, 1980. Ages 4–7.

Aruego, José. *Look What I Can Do,* illustrated by author. New York: Charles Scribner's Sons, 1971. Ages 3–6.

Association for Childhood Education International. *Sung Under the Silver Umbrella,* illustrated by Dorothy Lathrop. New York: Macmillan, 1972. Ages 3–8.

Bemelmans, Ludwig. *Madeline,* illustrated by author. New York: Viking Press, 1939. Ages 5–8.

———. *Madeline's Rescue.* New York: Viking Press, 1953. Ages 5–8.

Berger, Terry. *I Have Feelings.* New York: Human Sciences Press, 1980. Ages 4–8.

Beskow, Elsa. *Pelle's New Suit,* illustrated by author. New York: Harper & Brothers, 1929. Ages 3–6.

Bishop, Claire Huchet. *The Five Chinese Brothers,* illustrated by Kurt Wiese. New York: Coward, 1938. Ages 3–6.

Brown, Marcia, reteller. *Stone Soup: An Old Tale,* illustrated by reteller. New York: Charles Scribner's Sons, 1947. Ages 4–8.

Brown, Margaret Wise. *Goodnight Moon,* illustrated by Clement Hurd. New York: Harper & Brothers, 1947. Ages 3–6.

Buckley, Helen E. *Grandmother & I.* New York: Lothrop, Lee & Shepard, 1961. Ages 3–6.

Burningham, John. *Mr. Gumpy's Outing,* illustrated by author. New York: Holt, Rinehart & Winston, 1971. Ages 2–5.

———. *Seasons.* Indianapolis, Ind.: Bobbs-Merrill, 1971. Ages 2–5.

Burton, Virginia Lee. *Mike Mulligan and His Steam Shovel,* illustrated by author. Boston: Houghton Mifflin, 1939. Ages 5–9.

———. *The Little House,* illustrated by author. Boston: Houghton Mifflin, 1942. Ages 5–9.

———. *Katy and the Big Snow,* illustrated by author. Boston: Houghton Mifflin, 1942. Ages 5–9.

———. *Maybelle the Cable Car,* illustrated by author. Boston: Houghton Mifflin, 1942. Ages 5–9.

Byars, Betsy. *Go and Hush the Baby,* illustrated by Emily A. McCully. New York: Viking Press, 1971. Ages 5 and up.

Carle, Eric. *Very Hungry Caterpillar,* illustrated by author. New York: Collins, 1969. Ages 2–4.

Castiglia, Julie. *Jill the Pill.* New York: Atheneum, 1979. Ages 3–6.

Clifton, Lucille. *Some of the Days of Everett Anderson,* illustrated by Evaline Ness. New York: Holt, Rinehart & Winston, 1970. Ages 5–7.

Cohen, Miriam. *Lost in the Museum,* illustrated by Lillian Hoban. New York: Greenwillow Books, 1979. Ages 5–7.

———. *When Will I Read?* New York: Greenwillow Books, 1977. Ages 5–7.

———. *Will I Have a Friend?* New York: Macmillan, 1967. Ages 4–6.

———. *New Teacher.* New York: Macmillan, 1974. Ages 4–6.

Collins, Patricia. *My Friend Andrew.* Englewood Cliffs, N.J.: Prentice-Hall, 1981. Ages 3–7.

Daugherty, James. *Andy and the Lion,* illustrated by author. New York: Viking Press, 1938. Ages 6–8.

DeBrunhoff, Jean. *Story of Babar,* illustrated by author. New York: Random House, 1937. Ages 4–8.

DePaola, Tomie. *Nana Upstairs and Nana Downstairs,* illustrated by author. New York: Putnam, 1973. Ages 4–8.

———. *Oliver Button Is a Sissy.* New York: Harcourt Brace Jovanovich, 1979. Ages 4–8.

———. *Andy: That's My Name.* Englewood Cliffs, N.J.: Prentice-Hall, 1973. Ages 4–8.

———. *Now One Foot, Now the Other.* New York: Putnam, 1981. Ages 4–8.

De Regniers, Beatrice Schenk. *Snow Party,* illustrated by Reiner Zimnik. New York: Pantheon, 1959. Ages 4–7.

———. *May I Bring a Friend?,* illustrated by Beni Montresor. New York: Atheneum, 1964. Ages 4–7.

Duvoisin, Roger. *Petunia,* illustrated by author. New York: Alfred A. Knopf, 1950. Ages 4–7.

———. *Petunia Takes a Trip.* New York: Alfred A. Knopf, 1953. Ages 5–8.

Emberley, Barbara. *Drummer Hoff.* Illustrated by Ed Emberley. Englewood Cliffs, N.J.: Prentice-Hall, 1967. Ages 5 and up.

Ets, Marie Hall. *Just Me,* illustrated by author. New York: Viking Press, 1965. Ages 5–8.

Fatio, Louise. *The Happy Lion,* illustrated by Roger Duvoisin. New York: McGraw-Hill, 1954. Ages 5–8.

Flack, Marjorie. *Ask Mr. Bear,* illustrated by author. New York: Macmillan, 1971. Ages 5–6.

———. *The Story About Ping,* illustrated by Kurt Wiese. New York: Viking Press, 1933. Ages 4–9.

Freeman, Don. *Corduroy,* illustrated by author. New York: Viking Press, 1968. Ages 4–6.

Gag, Wanda. *Millions of Cats,* illustrated by author. New York: Coward, 1938. Ages 5–7.

———. *ABC Bunny,* illustrated by author. New York: Coward, 1933. Ages 5–7.

Gauch, Patricia Lee. *Grandpa & Me.* New York: Coward, McCann & Geoghegan, 1972. Ages 5–8.

Geisel, Theodor Seuss. *The 500 Hats of Bartholomew Cubbins.* New York: Vanguard, 1938. Ages 3–6.

Gramatky, Hardie. *Little Toot,* illustrated by author. New York: Putnam, 1939. Ages 4–7.

Hader, Berta and Elmer. *The Big Snow,* illustrated by authors. New York: Macmillan, 1948. Ages 6–8.

Haley, Gail E., reteller. *A Story—A Story,* illustrated by reteller. New York: Atheneum, 1970. Ages 5–7.

Hoban, Russell. *Bedtime for Frances,* illustrated by Garth Williams. New York: Harper & Row, 1960. Ages 6–8.

Hoban, Tana. *Shapes and Things.* New York: Macmillan, 1970. Ages 2–5.

———. *Look Again.* New York: Macmillan, 1971. Ages 2–5.

Hutchins, Pat. *Changes, Changes,* illustrated by author. New York: Macmillan, 1971. Ages 3 and up.

———. *Rosie's Walk,* illustrated by author. New York: Macmillan, 1968. Ages 3–6.

"I and the Others" Writers Collective. *It's Scary Sometimes.* New York: Human Sciences Press, 1980. Ages 4–8.

Iverson, Genie. *I Want to Be Big.* New York: Unicorn, 1979. Ages 4–6.

Jarrell, Mary. *The Knee-Baby.* New York: Farrar, Straus & Giroux, 1973. Ages 3 and up.

Johnson, Crockett. *Harold and the Purple Crayon.* New York: Harper & Brothers, 1958. Ages 5–8.

Keats, Ezra Jack. *Peter's Chair,* illustrated by author. New York: Harper & Row, 1967. Ages 4–7.

———. *The Snowy Day.* New York: Viking Press, 1962. Ages 3–6.

———. *Whistle for Willie.* New York: Viking Press, 1964. Ages 3–6.

———. *Goggles.* New York: Macmillan, 1969. Ages 4–7.

———. *Hi Cat!.* New York: Macmillan, 1970. Ages 4–7.

———. *Maggie and the Pirate.* New York: Scholastic, 1979. Ages 4–7.

Langstaff, John. *Frog Went a Courtin',* illustrated by Feodor Rojankovsky. New York: Harcourt, Brace, 1955. Ages 4 and up.

Lionni, Leo. *Inch by Inch.* Stamford, CT.: Astor-Honor, 1960. Ages 3–6.

———. *Fredrick.* New York: Pantheon, 1967. Ages 3–6.

———. *Swimmy.* New York: Pantheon, 1963. Ages 3–6.

Lipkind, William. *Finders Keepers,* illustrated by Nicholas Mordvinoff. New York: Harcourt, Brace, 1951. Ages 5–7.

Little, Lessie, and Greenfield, Eloise. *I Can Do It by Myself,* illustrated by Carole Byard. New York: Crowell, 1978. Ages 4–6.

McCloskey, Robert. *Blueberries for Sal,* illustrated by author. New York: Viking Press, 1948. Ages 4–6.

———. *Lentil,* illustrated by author. New York: Viking Press, 1940. Ages 7–9.

———. *Make Way for Ducklings,* illustrated by author. New York: Viking Press, 1941. Ages 4–6.

———. *One Morning in Maine,* illustrated by author. New York: Viking Press, 1952. Ages 5–7.

MacDonald, Golden. *The Little Island,* illustrated by Leonard Weisgard. Garden City, N.Y.: Doubleday, 1971. Ages 5–7.

Merriam, Eve. *Boys and Girls and Boys.* New York: Holt, Rinehart & Winston, 1972. Ages 5–8.

Munari, Bruno. *Bruno Munari's ABC,* illustrated by author. New York: Collins, 1960. Ages 3–5.

Myers, Walter M. *Where Does the Day Go?,* New York: Parents' Magazine Press, 1969. Ages 4–7.

Ness, Evaline. *Do You Have The Time, Lydia?,* illustrated by author. New York: E. P. Dutton, 1971. Ages 4–7.

———. *Everett Anderson's Christmas Coming,* illustrated by author. New York: Holt, Rinehart & Winston, 1971. Ages 5 and up.

Nicleodhas, Sorche. *Always Room for One More,* illustrated by Nonny Hogrogian. New York: Holt, Rinehart & Winston, 1965. All ages.

Peet, Bill. *Ant and the Elephant.* Boston: Houghton Mifflin, 1972. Ages 5–8.

Perrault, Charles. *Little Red Riding Hood,* illustrated by William Stobbs. New York: Henry Z. Walck, 1973. Ages 6 and up.

Potter, Beatrix. *The Tale of Peter Rabbit,* illustrated by author. New York: Warne, 1903. Ages 3–6.

Prather, Ray. *Anthony & Sabrina.* New York: Macmillan, 1973. Ages 5–8.

Raskin, Ellen. *Nothing Evers Happens on My Block,* illustrated by author. New York: Atheneum, 1966. Ages 5–8.

Rey, H. A. *Curious George,* illustrated by author. Boston: Houghton Mifflin, 1941. Ages 5–8.

Rockwell, Harlow. *Doctor.* New York: Macmillan, 1973. Ages 5–6.

―――. *Dentist.* New York: Greenwillow Books, 1975. Ages 5–7.

―――. *Nursery School.* New York: Greenwillow Books, 1976. Ages 5–8.

Rogers, Fred. *Mister Rogers Talks About the New Baby, Moving . . . Haircuts.* New York: Platt & Munk, 1974. Ages 2–6.

Rojankovsky, Feodor. *The Tall Book of Mother Goose,* illustrated by author. New York: Harper & Row, 1942. Ages 2–6.

―――. *Animals on the Farm,* illustrated by author. New York: Alfred A. Knopf, 1967. Ages 3–6.

Ruffins, Reynold. *My Brother Never Feeds the Cat.* New York: Charles Scribner's Sons, 1979. Ages 4–7.

Sawyer, Ruth. *Journey Cake, Ho!,* illustrated by Robert McCloskey. New York: Viking Press, 1953. Ages 4–8.

Schmiderer, Dorothy. *The Alphabeast Book: An Abecedarium,* illustrated by author. New York: Holt, Rinehart & Winston, 1971. Ages preschool–8.

Sendak, Maurice. *Where the Wild Things Are,* illustrated by author. New York: Harper & Row, 1963. Ages 5–8.

Seuss, Dr. *And to Think I Saw It on Mulberry Street,* illustrated by author. New York: Random House, 1937. Ages 5–9.

―――. *Horton Hatches the Egg.* New York: Random House, 1940. Ages 5–9.

―――. *Thidwick, the Big-Hearted Moose.* New York: Random House, 1948. Ages 5–9.

Simon, Norma. *What Do I Say?,* illustrated by Joe Lasker. Chicago: Albert Whitman, 1967. Ages 3–6.

―――. *How Do I Feel?,* Chicago: Albert Whitman, 1970. Ages 4–7.

―――. *I Was So Mad.* New York: David McKay, 1964. Ages 5–8.

Sonneborn, Ruth A. *Friday Night Is Papa Night.* New York: Macmillan, 1970. Ages 5–8.

Steig, William. *Sylvester and the Magic Pebble,* illustrated by author. New York: Windmill Books, 1969. Ages 5–7.

Steptoe, John. *Stevie,* illustrated by author. New York: Harper & Row, 1969. Ages 6–10.

Thurber, James. *Many Moons,* illustrated by Louis Slobodkin. New York: Harcourt, Brace, 1943. All ages.

Tresselt, Alvin. *White Snow, Bright Snow,* illustrated by Roger

Duvoisin. New York: Lothrop, Lee & Shepard, 1947. Ages 5–7.

———. *The Beaver Pond,* illustrated by Roger Duvoisin. New York: Lothrop, Lee & Shepard, 1970. Ages 4–8.

Udry, Janice May. *A Tree Is Nice,* illustrated by Marc Simont. New York: Harper & Brothers, 1956. Ages 5–8.

———. *Let's Be Enemies.* New York: Harper & Row, 1961. Ages 3–6.

Ungerer, Tomi. *Crictor,* illustrated by author. New York: Harper & Row, 1958. Ages 4–8.

Viorst, Judith. *Alexander and the Terrible, Horrible, No Good, Very Bad Day.* New York: Atheneum, 1976. Ages 5–8.

———. *My Mom Says There Aren't Any Zombies, Ghosts, Vampires, Creatures, Demons, Monsters, Friends, Goblins or Things.* New York: Atheneum, 1973. Ages 5–9.

———. *The 10th Good Thing About Barney.* New York: Atheneum, 1972. Ages 5–9.

Waber, Bernard. *Lyle, Lyle, Crocodile.* Boston: Houghton Mifflin, 1965. Ages 3–5.

———. *Ira Sleeps Over.* Boston: Houghton Mifflin, 1972. Ages 3–7.

Ward, Lynd. *The Biggest Bear,* illustrated by author. Boston: Houghton Mifflin, 1952. Ages 5–8.

Wildsmith, Brian. *Brian Wildsmith's ABC,* illustrated by author. New York: Franklin Watts, 1962. Ages 3–6.

Yashima, Taro and Mitsu. *Crow Boy,* illustrated by author. New York: Viking Press, 1955. Ages 7–9.

Zolotow, Charlotte. *A Tiger Called Thomas.* New York: Lothrop, Lee & Shepard, 1963. Ages 4–7.

———. *Janey.* New York: Harper & Row, 1973. Ages 4–7.

———. *William's Doll.* New York: Harper & Row, 1971. Ages 4–7.

———. *The Quarrelling Book.* New York: Harper & Row, 1963. Ages 4–7.

———. *Big Sister—Little Sister.* New York: Harper & Row, 1966. Ages 3–7.

———. *A Father Like That.* New York: Harper & Row, 1971. Ages 4–7.

———. *Do You Know What I'll Do?* New York: Harper & Row, 1958. Ages 3–7.

Books for Primary-School-Age Children

Bonsall, Crosby N. *It's Mine! A Greedy Book.* New York: Harper & Row, 1964. Ages 4–7.

Brenner, Barbara. *Mr. Tall and Mr. Small.* Glenview, Ill.: Young Scott Books, 1966. Ages 4–8.

Bridwell, Norman. *Clifford Takes a Trip.* New York: Scholastic, 1966. Ages 4–8.

————. *Clifford's Good Deeds*. New York: Scholastic, 1975. Ages 4–8.

Brown, Myra Berry. *Sandy Signs His Name*. New York: Franklin Watts, 1967. Ages 6–8.

Cleary, Beverly. *Henry Huggins,* illustrated by Louis Darling. New York: William Morrow, 1950. Ages 8–9.

————. *Ramona the Pest*, illustrated by Louis Darling. New York: William Morrow, 1968. Ages 8–10.

Cooney, Barbara, reteller. *Chanticleer and the Fox,* illustrated by reteller. New York: Crowell, 1958. Ages 6–11.

Dalgliesh, Alice. *The Columbus Story,* illustrated by Leo Politi. New York: Charles Scribner's Sons, Ages 8–10.

Delton, Judy. *Two Good Friends*. New York: Crown, 1954. Ages 5–7.

————. *The New Girl at School*. New York: E. P. Dutton, 1979. Ages 5–7.

Fassler, Joan. *Howie Helps Himself*. Chicago: Albert Whitman, 1974. Ages 5–8.

————. *One Little Girl*. New York: Human Sciences Press, 1980. Ages 5–8.

Fedar, Paula Kurzband. *Where Does the Teacher Live?* New York: E. P. Dutton, 1979. Ages 6–8.

Gaeddert, Lou Ann. *Noisy Nancy Norris*. New York: Doubleday, 1965. Ages 6–8.

Guilfoile, Elizabeth. *Nobody Listens to Andrew,* illustrated by Mary Stevens. Chicago: Follett, 1957. Ages 6–8.

Hickman, Martha Whitmore. *I'm Moving*. Nashville, Tenn.: Abingdon Press, 1974. Ages 5–8.

Hill, Elizabeth S. *Evan's Corner*. New York: Holt, Rinehart & Winston, 1967. Ages 6–9.

Hoff, Syd. *Who Will Be My Friends?* New York: Harper & Row, 1960. Ages 5–7.

Hughes, Shirley. *Moving Molly*. Englewood Cliffs, N.J.: Prentice-Hall, 1978. Ages 7–9.

Kraus, Robert. *The Littlest Rabbit*. New York: Harper & Row, 1961. Ages 4–7.

————. *Amanda Remembers*. New York: Harper & Row, 1965. Ages 4–7.

————. *Leo the Late Bloomer*. New York: Windmill Books, 1971. Ages 4–7.

Leaf, Munro. *The Story of Ferdinand,* illustrated by Robert Lawson. New York: Viking Press, 1936. Ages 5 and up.

————. *The Boy Who Would Not Go to School: Robert Francis Weatherbee*. New York: Scholastic, 1963. Ages 5–8.

Levine, Edna. *Lisa and Her Soundless Word*. New York: Human Sciences Press, 1980. Ages 5–9.

Lexau, Joan. *I Should Have Stayed in Bed,* illustrated by Syd Hoff. New York: Harper & Row, 1965. Ages 6–7.

Lobel, Arnold. *Days with Frog and Toad,* illustrated by author. New York: Harper & Row, 1976. Ages 5–7.

———. *Frog and Toads Are Friends,* illustrated by author. New York: Harper & Row, 1972. Ages 5–7.

Maestro, Betty. *Harriet Reads Signs and More Signs.* New York: Crown, 1980. Ages 5–8.

Marshall, James. *George and Martha,* illustrated by author. Boston: Houghton Mifflin, 1972. Ages 5–8.

Martin, Bill, Jr. *David Was Mad.* New York: Holt, Rinehart & Winston, 1967. Ages 4–7.

McCloskey, Robert. *Time of Wonder,* illustrated by author. New York: Viking Press, 1948. Ages 6–10.

Milne, A. A. *Winnie the Pooh,* illustrated by Ernest Shepard. New York: E. P. Dutton, 1974. Ages 6–11.

Milord, Sue. *Maggie and the Good-bye Gift.* New York: Lothrop, Lee & Shepard, 1979. Ages 4–7.

Minarik, Else. *Little Bear,* illustrated by Maurice Sendak. New York: Harper & Brothers, 1957. Ages 5–7.

Parish, Peggy. *Amelia Bedelia,* illustrated by Fritz Siebel. New York: Harper & Row, 1963. Ages 6–8.

———. *Play Ball, Amelia Bedelia,* illustrated by Wallace Tripp. New York: Harper & Row, 1972. Ages 7–9.

———. *Dinosaur Time,* illustrated by Arnold Lobel. New York: Harper & Row, 1974. Ages 6–8.

Preston, Edna Mitchell. *The Temper Tantrum Book.* New York: Viking Press, 1976. Ages 4–8.

Raskin, Ellen. *Spectacles.* New York: Atheneum, 1968. Ages 5–9.

Tobias, Tobi. *Petey.* New York: Putnam, 1978. Ages 5–9.

———. *Moving Day.* New York: Alfred A. Knopf, 1976. Ages 5–7.

Warbug, Sandal S. *Growing Time.* Boston: Houghton Mifflin, 1969. Ages 7–9.

Willard, Nancy. *Simple Pictures Are Best.* New York: Harcourt Brace Jovanovich, 1976. Ages 6–10.

Wolf, Bernard. *Don't Feel Sorry for Paul.* Philadelphia: J. B. Lippincott, 1974. Ages 8 and up.

Zion, Gene. *The Plant Sitter.* New York: Harper & Row, 1959. Ages 4–8.

———. *Harry, the Dirty Dog.* New York: Harper & Row, 1956. Ages 4–7.

Joke and Riddle Books

Alley, R. W., illus. *The Silly Riddle Book.* Racine, Wis.: Western, 1981. Ages 3–6.

Beard, Isobel R. *Puzzles & Riddles.* Chicago: Follett, 1982. Ages 3–6.

Carlson, Bernice W. *Funny Bones Dramatics*. Nashville, Tenn.:
  Abingdon Press, 1974. Ages 5–8.
Cole, William, *The Book of Giggles*. New York: Dell, 1981. Ages 5
  and up.
Highlights Editors. *Jokes from Highlights*. Columbus, O.:
  Highlights for Children, 1969. Ages 7 and up.
Kohl, Marguerite, and Young, Fredrica. *Jokes for Children*. New
  York: Hill & Wang, 1963. Ages 7 and up.
Leonard, Marcia, and Cricket Magazine Editors. *Cricket's Jokes,
  Riddles and Other Stuff*. New York: Random House, 1977.
  Ages 6 and up.
Low, Joseph. *Five Men Under One Umbrella*. New York: Macmillan,
  1975. Ages 6–8.
Moore, Eva. *Lucky Book of Riddles*. New York: Scholastic, 1969.
  Ages 5–8.
Rosenbloom, Joseph. *Biggest Riddle Book in the World*. New York:
  Sterling, 1976. Ages 7 and up.
———. *Monster Madness: Riddles, Jokes and Fun*. New York:
  Sterling, 1980. Ages 7 and up.
Sarnoff, Jane, and Ruffins, Reynold. *The Monster Riddle Book*. New
  York: Charles Scribner's Sons, 1975. Ages 6 and up.
———. *I Know! A Riddle Book*. New York: Charles Scribner's Sons,
  1976. Ages 6 and up.
Schwartz, Alvin. *Ten Copycats in a Boat and Other Riddles*. New
  York: Harper & Row, 1980. Ages 5–8.
———. *A Twister of Twists, A Tangler of Tongues*. New York:
  Harper & Row, 1972. Ages 5 and up.
Sesame Street. *Sesame Street Pop-Up Riddle Book*. New York:
  Random House, 1977. Ages 3–8.
Thaler, Mike. *Oinkers Away: Pig Riddles, Cartoons, and Jokes*. New
  York: Archway, 1981. Ages 6 and up.
Underwood, Ralph. *Ask Me Another Riddle*. New York: Grosset and
  Dunlap Publishers, 1964. Ages 5–8.
Walt Disney Productions. *Jokes & Riddles*. Racine, Wis.: Western,
  1980. Ages 3–8.
Zimmerman, Andrea. *The Riddle Zoo*. New York: E. P. Dutton,
  1981. Ages 8 and up.

APPENDIX B
SELECTED FREE OR INEXPENSIVE
MATERIALS FOR PARENTS

Action for Children's Television
46 Austin Street
Newtonville, MA 02160

Send a nine-inch self-addressed stamped envelope with two first-class stamps and ask for a poster entitled "Treat TV with T.L.C." You can also send $1.00 and ask for a special red-and-white "TV Reminder Tag" for the TV set.

American Library Association
Public Information Office/Reading Begins at Home—FSFP
50 East Huron Street
Chicago, IL 60611

Send a nine-inch self-addressed stamped envelope and ask for a brochure entitled *Reading Begins at Home.*

American Occupational Therapy Foundation
Dept. FS
1383 Piccard Drive, Suite 201
Rockville, MD 20850

Send $.25 with your request for a booklet entitled *The Child with Minimal Brain Dysfunction.*

American Optometric Association, Communications Division
243 North Lindbergh Boulevard
St. Louis, MO 63141

Send a self-addressed stamped envelope and ask for the brochures entitled *Facts You Should Know About Vision and School* and *A Parent's Guide to Vision Problems of Young Children.*

Association for Childhood Education International
3615 Wisconsin Avenue, N.W.
Washington, DC 20016

Write for a free copy of the list of ACEI publications available through the association.

Asthma and Allergy Foundation of America
19 West 44th Street
New York, NY 10036

Send $.50 and request a pamphlet entitled *Food Allergy*. Send a postcard and request a free brochure entitled *Questions and Answers About Asthma and Allergy Diseases*.

Children's Television Workshop
Community Education Services/Dept. FS
1 Lincoln Plaza
New York, NY 10023

Send $1.00 and ask for the twenty-six-page booklet entitled *The Muppet Gallery*. This booklet comes in English or Spanish. Specify which you prefer.

Consumer Information Center
Dept. 106H
Pueblo, CO 81009

Three items that may be of interest to parents are:
1. A reprint entitled *Children and Television*. To obtain this reprint send a postcard requesting it.
2. A brochure entitled *Plain Talk About Children with Learning Disabilities*. To obtain this brochure send a postcard requesting it.
3. Send $1.00 and request a booklet entitled *Beautiful Junk*.

Council for Exceptional Children
1920 Association Drive
Reston, VA 22091

1. Send $1.00 and request a packet entitled *Parents of Handicapped Children Packet*.
2. Send $1.00 and request a packet entitled *Parents of Gifted Children Packet*.

CTB/McGraw-Hill
Parent's Guide, Box FSP
Del Monte Research Park
Monterey, CA 93940

Send a nine-inch self-addressed stamped envelope and ask for a free copy of *Parent's Guide to Understanding Tests*.

> Gryphon House Publications Delivery Service
> P.O. Box 246
> 3706 Otis Street
> Mt. Rainier, MD 20822

Parents can write for a free copy of an annual *Publications Catalog*, which lists resources for child care.

> Division of Childhood and Parenting
> Appalachia Educational Laboratory, Inc.
> P.O. Box 1348
> Charleston, WV 25325

Write for a free copy of a brochure entitled *Aids to Early Learning*.

> Nancy Everhart
> Baby Book
> 224 Catawissa Street
> Tamaqua, PA 18252

Send $1.00 and request a booklet entitled *100 Ways to Entertain Your Baby*.

> *The Exceptional Parent*
> 20 Providence Street, Suite 700
> Boston, MA 02116

Send $1.00 and request a sample copy of the magazine *The Exceptional Parent*.

> Hedstrom Co.
> Dept. FSFP
> Sunnside Road
> Bedford, PA 15522

Send $1.00 and request a booklet entitled *Priceless Pointers for Parents of Growing Children*.

> The Home and School Institute, Inc.
> c/o Trinity College
> Washington, DC 20017
> Attn.: Publications

Write for a brochure that lists books and prices of the publications available through The Home and School Institute.

Horn Book
31 St. James Avenue
Boston, MA 02116

Write for information about the *Horn Book* magazine.

International Reading Association
800 Barksdale Road
P.O. Box 8139
Newark, DE 19711

Send a No. 10 self-addressed stamped envelope (one-ounce first-class postage) and request a single copy of five easy-to-read brochures: (1) *Good Books Make Reading Fun for Your Child,* (2) *Summer Reading is Important,* (3) *You Can Encourage Your Child to Read,* (4) *You Can Use Television to Stimulate Your Child's Reading Habits,* and (5) *Your Home Is Your Child's First School.* Also, send $.50 and request a booklet entitled *How Does My Child's Vision Affect His Reading?*

National Assessment Distribution Center
700 Lincoln Tower
1860 Lincoln Street
Denver, CO 80295

Send a postcard and request a question-and-answer brochure with a set of foldouts on the subject of assessment.

National Association for the Education of Young Children
1834 Connecticut Avenue, N.W.
Washington, DC 20009

Inquire about *Young Children,* a publication produced bimonthly.

National Association for Gifted Children
2070 County Road H
St. Paul, MN 55112

Send $1.00 and request the *Parent Packet on Giftedness.*

National Citizens Committee for Broadcasting
P.O. Box 12038
Washington, DC 20005

Send a nine-inch self-addressed stamped envelope and ask for a reprint entitled *How Television Affects Your Child.*

NCMHI, National Institute of Mental Health
Public Inquiries, Room 11A-21
5600 Fishers Lane
Rockville, MD 20857

Send a postcard and request a booklet entitled *Yours, Mine & Ours: Tips for Stepparents.* You can also request a booklet entitled *Dyslexia.*

National Council of Teachers of English (NCTE)
1111 Kenyon Road
Urbana, IL 61801

Write for a free brochure entitled *How to Help Your Child Become a Better Writer.*

National Organization of Mothers of Twins Clubs (NOMOTC)
5402 Amberwood Lane
Rockville, MD 20853

Send a postcard and ask for a reprint entitled *Your Twins and You.*

National Society to Prevent Blindness
Dept. FSFP
79 Madison Avenue
New York, NY 10016

Send a nine-inch self-addressed stamped envelope and request four brochures: (1) *First Aid for Eye Emergencies,* (2) *Home Eye Test for Preschoolers,* (3) *Crossed Eyes: A Needless Handicap,* and (4) *Signs of Possible Eye Trouble in Children.*

The Orton Society
8415 Bellona Lane, Dept. P
Towson, MD 21204

Send a postcard and request a booklet on The Orton Society.

Our Baby's First Seven Years
5841 South Maryland Avenue
Dept. FS
Chicago, IL 60637

Send $.30 and request a booklet entitled *The Nature and Nuture of Infants.*

Parents Without Partners, Inc.
7910 Woodmont Avenue
Dept. MP
Washington, DC 20014

Send $.50 per foldout and request three foldouts entitled (1) *The Single Parent,* (2) *Are You a Single Parent?,* and (3) *Single-Parent Resources.* Also, you can order a sample copy of the brochure *The Single Parent* by enclosing $1.00 to defray costs.

Prime Time School Television
Attn.: Free Stuff
120 South La Salle Street
Chicago, IL 60603

Send $1.00 and request a study guide entitled *Prime Time School Television Study Guide*.

Public Affairs Committee, Inc.—MP
381 Park Avenue South, Room 1101
New York, NY 10016

Send $.50 and ask for a booklet entitled *Your First Months with Your First Baby*.

Toy Manufacturers of America
Public Relations Dept.—Pamphlets
200 Fifth Avenue
New York, NY 10010

Send a postcard and request four pamphlets: (1) *Playing Safely with Toys*, (2) *Parents are the First Playmates*, (3) *Choosing Toys for Children*, and (4) *Toys Are Teaching Tools*.

Virginia Polytechnic Institute and State University
Blacksburg, VA 24060

Write for publication No. 721, *Winning Ways to Talk with Young Children*, by Dr. Betsy R. Scheneck.

APPENDIX C
MAGAZINES AND NEWSLETTERS FOR PARENTS

Magazines

Childhood Education (infancy to early adolescence)
Association for Childhood Education International
3615 Wisconsin Avenue, N.W.
Washington, DC 20016

Children Today (school age)
U.S. Children's Bureau
Administration for Children, Youth, and Families
U.S. Department of Education
Superintendent of Documents
Washington, DC 20402

Children's House (young children)
Children's House, Inc.
Box 111
Caldwell, NJ 07006

Children's World
Children's Hospital Medical Center
Public Relations Dept.
300 Longwood Avenue
Boston, MA 02115

Early Years (preschool and primary grades)
Allen Raymond, Inc.
P.O. Box 912
Farmingdale, NY 11735

Learning (school age)
Education Today Company, Inc.
Thomas O. Ryder
530 University Avenue
Palo Alto, CA 94301

Parents' (crib to college)
Parents' Magazine Enterprises, Inc.
52 Vanderbilt Avenue
New York, NY 10017

Puppetry Journal (nursery school and up)
Puppeteers of America
c/o Don Avery, Editor
2015 Novem Drive
Fenton, MO 63026

Newsletters

Association for Children with Learning Disabilities
4156 Library Road
Pittsburgh, PA 15234

Send a nine-inch self-addressed, stamped envelope and ask for a sample copy of *ACLD Newsbriefs.*

Building Blocks
Dept. 101
314 Liberty—P.O.Box 31
Dundee, IL 60118

Send $.50 and ask for a sample copy of *Building Blocks.*

Center for Parent Education
55 Chapel Street
Newton, MA 02160

Send a postcard asking about the newsletter and other services.

Gifted Children Newsletter
Subscription Dept. A
530 University Avenue
Palo Alto, CA 94301

Send $1.00 and ask for a sample copy of the *Gifted Children Newsletter.*

International Association of Parents of the Deaf
814 Thayer Avenue
Silver Spring, MD 20910

Send a postcard and ask for a sample copy of *The Endeavor; Moms & Pops & Kids;* and a catalog of publications.

International Reading Association
800 Barksdale Road
P.O. Box 8139
Newark, DE 19711

Send a nine-inch self-addressed stamped envelope and ask for the newsletter *News for Parents from IRA*.

Send a nine-inch self-addressed stamped envelope and ask for a reprint of *Practical Parenting*.

Meadowbrook Press
P.O. Box 638, FPS
Wayzata, MN 55391

Send a nine-inch self-addressed envelope and ask for a reprint entitled *Practical Parenting*.

Newsletter of Parenting
Dept. FW
2300 West Fifth Avenue
P.O. Box 2505
Columbus, OH 43216

Send a self-addressed stamped envelope and ask for a sample copy of *Newsletter of Parenting*.

Nurturing News
187 Caselli Ave.
San Francisco, CA 94114

Send a nine-inch self-addressed stamped envelope and ask for a sample copy of *Nurturing News*.

Parenting Center
92nd Street "Y"
1395 Lexington Avenue
New York, NY 10028

Send a postcard and ask for a sample copy of *Parenting Center Newsletter*.

Parents' Choice Foundation
Box 185
Waban, MA 02168

Write for a sample copy of *Parents' Choice Newsletter*.

Seattle's Child
P.O. Box 15107
Seattle, WA 98115

Send a postcard and ask for a sample copy of *Seattle's Child*.

Village Circle
P.O. Box 5361
Orange, CA 92667

Send $.30 and ask for a sample copy of the newsletter *Village Circle*.

Warren Publishing
1004 Harborview Lane
Everett, WA 98203

Send $.30 for a sample copy of the newsletter *Totline*.

APPENDIX D
ORGANIZATIONS FOR PARENTS

Alexander Graham Bell Association for the Deaf
3417 Volta Place, N.W.
Washington, DC 20007

An organization of teachers of the deaf, speech-language pathologists and audiologists, physicians, hearing-aid dealers, and all others interested in the problems of hearing impairment.

Publications:
Books and brochures about hearing impairment, and a monthly magazine called *The Volta Review*.

American Association of University Women
National Headquarters
2401 Virginia Avenue., N.W.
Washington, DC 20037

An association of women graduates of regionally accredited colleges and universities. Works for advancement of women, education, and lifelong learning.

Publications:
Write for information about the Families and Work programs.

American Foundation for the Blind
15 West 16th Street
New York, NY 10011

The foundation is a private, national organization whose objective is to help those who are visually handicapped to achieve the fullest possible development and utilization of their capacities and integration into the social, cultural, and economic life of the community. The organization serves as a clearinghouse for information about visual handicaps.

Publications:
The Journal of Visual Impairment and Blindness and other publications.

American Speech and Hearing Association
10801 Rockville Pike
Rockville, MD 20852

The association disseminates information on speech, language, and hearing and their disorders.

Publications:
Books and pamphlets as well as professional reports, monographs, and four journals: *ASHA* (monthly), *Journal of Speech and Hearing Disorders* (quarterly), *Journal of Speech and Hearing Research* (quarterly), and *Language, Speech, and Hearing Services in the Schools* (quarterly).

Association for Childhood Education International
3615 Wisconsin Avenue, N.W.
Washington, DC 20016

An organization of teachers, parents, and other adults interested in promoting good educational practices for children from infancy through early adolescence.

Publications:
Childhood Education, bulletins, bibliography of books for children, and leaflets on varied topics.

Association for the Education of the Visually Handicapped
919 Walnut Street
Philadelphia, PA 19107

An organization of teachers, administrators, parents, houseparents of blind children, schools, and others interested in the education, guidance, vocational rehabilitation, or occupational placement of the blind or partially seeing.

Publications:
Education of the Visually Handicapped (quarterly), *Fountainhead* (quarterly bulletin), *Convention Selected Papers* (biennial).

Black Child Development Institute
1028 Connecticut Avenue, N.W.
Washington, DC 20036

The institute seeks to ensure that black children and youth develop to their fullest potential.

Publications:
Black Child Advocate (quarterly newsletter); *Calendar* (annual); *Black*

Flash (irregular); also publishes research reports and seminar proceedings.

Children's Book Council
67 Irving Place
New York, NY 10003

A publishers' association encouraging the reading and enjoyment of children's books. Official sponsor of National Children's Book Week.

Publications:
Calendar (irregular); also publishes information sheets, bibliographies, brochures, and other educational and promotional materials for parents, teachers, librarians, and booksellers.

Closer Look
Box 1492
Washington, DC 20013

This special project attempts to provide bridges between parents and services for handicapped children, and to help parents become advocates for comprehensive services for their own handicapped child as well as for other handicapped children.

Publications:
A newsletter as well as information of special interest to parents of handicapped children.

Council on Interracial Books for Children
Racism/Sexism Resource Center
1841 Broadway
New York, NY 10023

The council promotes children's books and other materials which do not project a bias based on race, sex, age, or physical handicap.

Publications:
Bulletin, eight per year.

International Association of Parents of the Deaf
814 Thayer Avenue
Silver Spring, MD 20910

This association provides information about deafness to parents and the general public and refers parents to local contacts when appropriate.

Publications:
A newsletter, *Endeavor,* is published six times a year.

International Parents' Organization
Alexander Graham Bell Association for the Deaf

3417 Volta Place, N.W.
Washington, DC 20007

A parents' section of the Alexander Graham Bell Association for the Deaf.

Publications:
Newsletters, *The Volta Review,* and *Newsounds.*

Library of Congress
Division for the Blind and Physically Handicapped
Reference Department
Washington, DC 20542

The Division for the Blind and Physically Handicapped administers a national program providing free library service to persons who are unable to read standard print materials because of visual or physical impairment.

Publications:
Talking Book Topics (periodical), *DBPH News* (newsletter), and *Volunteers Who Produce Books* (directory).

National Association for Hearing and Speech Action
814 Thayer Avenue
Silver Spring, MD 20910

This is a private, nonprofit organization that works exclusively on behalf of hearing-, speech-, and language-handicapped individuals.

Publications:
A pamphlet, *So Your Child Has a Hearing Problem.*

National Citizens Committee for Broadcasting
P.O. Box 12038
Washington, DC 20005
Attn.: Sally Steenland

"A citizen-supported nonprofit organization whose purpose is to improve the quality of broadcasting through concerned public action."

Publications:
Access, Journal of Telecommunications Reform (biweekly); *Media Watch* (quarterly); *Citizens Media Directory* (irregular); also publishes *How to Talk Back to the Telephone Company.*

National Congress of Parents and Teachers
700 North Rush Street
Chicago, IL 60611

An organization of parents, teachers, students, principals, administrators, and others interested in uniting the forces of home, school, and community on behalf of children and youth.

Publications:
PTA Today, seven a year; also publishes *What's Happening in Washington* (newsletter) and materials on present education, television's effect on children, and other materials.

National Easter Seal Society for Crippled Children and Adults
2023 West Ogden Avenue
Chicago, IL 60612

The society provides services for disabled persons of all ages with orthopedic, neurological, or neuromuscular disabilities; sensory communication and learning disorders; or psychological or social dysfunction.

Publications:
A publications catalog; a professional journal, *Rehabilitation Literature.*

National Society for the Prevention of Blindness, Inc.
79 Madison Avenue
New York, NY 10016

The society provides services which include community service; publications; public, lay, and professional education; and basic clinical and operational research on visual handicaps.

Publications:
A preschool vision kit; *The Sight Saving Review* (quarterly).

The following resources were used to compile Appendices A–D:

Association for Childhood Education International. *Bibliography of Books for Children.* Washington, D.C.: The Association, 1977.
Encyclopedia of Associations, Vol. 1, 16th Ed. Detroit: Gale Research Company, 1981.
The Free Stuff Editors. *Free Stuff For Parents.* Deephaven, Minn.: Meadowbrook Press, 1980.
Head Start Bureau. *Mainstreaming Preschoolers: Children with Hearing Impairments.* Washington, D.C.: U.S. Department of Education, 78-31116.
———. *Mainstreaming Preschoolers: Children with Visual Handicaps.* Washington, D.C.: U.S. Department of Education, 78-31112.
———. *Mainstreaming Preschoolers: Children with Learning Disabilities.* Washington, D.C.: U.S. Department of Education, 79-31117.
Ulrich's International Periodicals Directory, 20th Ed. New York: R. R. Bowker Company, 1981.

Index